THE SECRET LIFE OF THE
EXPECTANT MOTHER

THE SECRET LIFE OF THE EXPECTANT MOTHER

Nine Months of Mysterious Intuitions
and Heightened Perceptions

CARL JONES

A CITADEL PRESS BOOK
PUBLISHED BY CAROL PUBLISHING GROUP

A Citadel Press Book
Published by Carol Publishing Group
Citadel Press is a registered trademark of Carol Communications, Inc.

Editorial, sales and distribution, rights and permissions inquiries should be addressed to Carol Publishing Group, 120 Enterprise Avenue, Secaucus, N.J. 07094

In Canada: Canadian Manda Group, One Atlantic Avenue, Suite 105, Toronto, Ontario M6K 3E7

Carol Publishing books may be purchased in bulk special discounts for sales promotion, fund-raising, or educational purposes. Special editions can be created to specifications. For details, contact Special Sales Department, 120 Enterprise Avenue, Secaucus, N.J. 07094.

Manufactured in the United States of America
10 9 8 7 6 5 4 3 2 1

Library of Congress Cataloging-in-Publication Data
Jones, Carl.
    The secret life of the expectant mother : nine months of
mysterious intuitions and heightened perceptions / Carl Jones.
        p.   cm.
    "A Citadel Press book."
    Includes index.
    ISBN 0-8065-1938-X (pbk.)
    1. Extrasensory perception.   2. Intuition (Psychology)   3. Pregnant
women—Miscellanea.   4. Pregnancy—Miscellanea.   I. Title.
BF1321.J67   1997
133.8'085'2—dc21   97-22322
                                                                                   CIP

CONTENTS

INTRODUCTION

After leading a guided imagery exercise with a group of women, an expectant mother told me she knew her unborn child was a boy with brown eyes.

"Have you had an ultrasound?" I asked her. The ultrasound would have shown the gender but not the brown eyes.

"No," the mother replied, her hand on her expanding belly, "I just know." She gave birth to a boy with brown eyes. It was my first glimpse of the secret world of expectant mothers. Later I learned all women share this secret world.

This realization led me on a research project involving thousands of expectant and new parents. And it brought me to a conclusion that could change the way we think of childbirth.

Many, if not all, expectant and new parents experience heightened intuition during the childbearing months. This book will later explain why expectant parents have a corner on ESP or "intuition." For now, the implications of the secret world of expectant mothers are staggering for health care professionals as well as parents.

A certified childbirth educator and author of many popular books, I began talking about pregnancy intuition in my workshops held for thousands of health professionals yearly. Many of them already knew about this hidden dimension of pregnancy. They just hadn't put it into words before.

I taught professionals how to reduce the fear and pain of labor without using drugs. I developed a program certifying labor companions (persons who comfort a woman through labor). Studies later showed that the presence of such persons has reduced the cesarean rate by one third and cut down the need for medication, thereby encouraging healthier mothers and healthier babies.

Medical professionals who themselves had given birth often ask me how I, being male, could describe so accurately the experience of labor. My answer was that everything I know about labor comes from the laboring mother; I pay attention to the laboring mother with my heart as well as with my cognitive mind. But what did this statement mean? I wasn't sure myself. I now realize it had something to do with intuition—an unconscious rapport with the laboring mother. Paying attention to that intuition led me to create the guided imagery exercises in *Mind Over Labor*—a book that shaped the way women give birth from Baltimore to Tokyo, that reduced laboring women's pain so dramatically that few asked for analgesia, and that put pregnant women in touch with their greatest resource: the inner self.

In addition to training health professionals, I've worked with hundreds of laboring women and breast-feeding mothers. Now that I'm aware of it, I see the evidence of intuition almost daily. Occasionally it surfaces in dramatic episodes.

"I know something is wrong with my baby," a mother says, suddenly waking from a nightmare. She has an ultrasound, which finds that the umbilical cord is wrapped twice around the baby's neck. An emergency cesarean saves her baby's life.

Learning about the secret world of expectant mothers can open the door on a new way of looking at pregnancy and childbirth; it can make us more aware of the mystery of our beginnings; and it may save your child's life. Think about it.

The Secret Life of the Expectant Mother

CHAPTER 1

A Case of the Inexplicable

Nothing short of the voyages of Ulysses compares to the odyssey of sperm to greet egg.

Like a tadpole with a flat oval head, the sperm swims, whipping his tail from side to side. Like a tadpole but infinitely smaller. So small it has been said that enough sperm to fertilize all the women on earth could fit in the hull of a single grain of rice.

If this tiny "being" had eyes, he would see something remarkable when his journey began. For at the time the mother is most fertile, her cervical mucus undergoes a change. A bead of this mucus viewed under a microscope looks like a primeval fern forest. A gynecologist with a poetic turn of mind termed this fernlike effect "arborization."

Simultaneously, the cervical mucus becomes elastic. A drop between spread fingers becomes a clear elastic strand.

The microscopic seed journeys upward through the fern forest. He journeys through the tiny aperture of the cervix, through the uterus, and into one of the two fallopian tubes that connect the uterus to the egg-creating ovary. Here, in the narrow passage between ovary and womb, the egg waits.

She is a single cell, a minute speck like the point of a sharp pin. Yet to something the sperm's size, she is like an ocean. She is surrounded by two membranes and encircled by many small cells that have the appearance of flames leaping around the sun. The name for this layer of cells is *corona radiata,* or "rayed crown." The rayed crown resembles the mandalas of cultures from the ancient Indians to the Mayans. Mandalas are symbols of integration, wholeness. Like the union of sperm and egg.

A mysterious process takes place when the tiny traveler approaches the living mandala. A part of the sperm's head removes itself. It is as if the sperm were doffing his cap before the majesty of the rayed crown, paying homage. Biologically, an enzymatic substance from a part of the sperm's head called the *acrosome,* or "cap," triggers the cells to part and make way for him.

From the onlooker's point of view, could there be an onlooker, it must seem like something out of the Arabian Nights. The walls of the egg open. They make way for him. She helps him enter. She welcomes him. Then the universe changes, bursts into bloom like the great renewal of spring carpeting the earth.

There is a rushing motion like the meeting of two lovers greeting one another after a long absence. The sperm's slender tail vanishes. His head enlarges. He swims to the center of the egg. Then he dissolves, and the two become one. A tiny dot swirls in its own private universe. Conception. There are thousands of mothers and fathers who claim to know the very minute it happens, but can anyone really feel such a tiny process within the body?

Our first taste of the mystery of pregnancy happened on the night our oldest son, Carl, was conceived. There was nothing unusual about that night. No feelings of the uncanny.

My wife, Jan, and I had just made love. Almost immediately afterward, we sensed there was something different about that experience—something almost impossible to put into words. Call it a subtle inner glow, a sense of knowing. Neither my wife nor I are especially intuitive. However, simultaneously, we both realized a child had been conceived.

Patrick, a father in California, had a similar experience. "My wife and I had decided to try to make a baby," Patrick recalls. "One night, during lovemaking, I had the strongest feeling that we were doing just that. I seemed at some level to feel the creative forces merge to form a girl. So strong was this perception, immediately afterward, I leaped out of bed and wrote on the calendar, 'This night my baby girl was conceived.'

"Six weeks later the doctor told us that my wife was six weeks pregnant! All through the pregnancy I seemed aware at some level of my daughter, a connection that has persisted to this day (she's twelve now)."

Patrick's experience, though dramatic, is hardly unique.

Most women do not learn they are pregnant until several days if not weeks have passed. They miss a period or begin to feel physical changes.

THE SIGNS OF PREGNANCY

The most common signs of pregnancy include the following:

- A missed menstrual period
- Morning nausea
- Fatigue
- A frequent need to urinate
- Breast changes (such as tenderness)
- Darkening of the areola (area around nipple)
- A feeling of fullness
- Changes in vaginal wall color
- Increased vaginal secretion
- An intuition that conceptions has occurred

Of all of these signs intuition occurs first, even before the most sophisticated medical tests

The signs of pregnancy include a missed menstrual period; morning sickness (nausea); fatigue; a frequent need to urinate; breast changes such as tenderness, darkening of the areola (brown pigmented region around the nipple); a feeling of fullness; changes in vaginal wall color from pinkish to bluish violet; and increased vaginal secretion. Another sign is an intuition that conception has occurred.

Over a thousand years ago B.C., the ancient Egyptians based pregnancy testing on the effects of a woman's urine on the growth of wheat and barley. Today, pregnancy tests still examine the woman's urine. All testing reacts to the hormone *HCG* (human chorionic gonadotropin), produced by the developing placenta and found in both the mother's urine and blood.

A laboratory can use either the mother's blood or her urine to test for HCG. Home pregnancy tests are accurate about 95 percent of the time. They are not effective until nine to fourteen days after the last menstrual period or about three or more weeks after conception. Laboratory urine tests, done with more sophisticated equipment, can detect pregnancy about two weeks after the last menstrual period or about twenty days after conception. The most sophisticated lab blood tests called *radioimmunoassay* are accurate seven to ten days after conception.

A few years ago, a woman had to wait weeks after conception to find out accurately if she were pregnant. Today, if she really wants to know as soon as possible, she can have a blood test within a few days of conception, but never the same day.

However, many parents know instantly. Immediately or within a few hours after making love, the conception intuition seems to provide an inner knowledge that pregnancy has occurred.

Wendy's experience is a typical example. "The day after I conceived, I knew I was pregnant," recalls Wendy, a mother of six in Orlando, Florida. It wasn't the right time of the month because there is no right time of the month for Wendy. Her periods are irregular and she ovulates at different times each cycle. But Wendy knew within twelve hours of lovemaking that she was pregnant.

Even more incredible, Vincent, her husband, sensed a child had been conceived before Wendy did. "Within five minutes of making love," he recalls, "I suddenly had a distinct realization."

When Wendy broke the exciting news to her husband, Vincent replied: "I already knew but I didn't want to shock you by telling you!"

Though there is no physiological reason either parent should know conception occurred within minutes of lovemaking, many mothers and fathers take the conception intuition for granted. For them, it is as much a part of pregnancy as tingling breasts. They view the intuition as part and parcel of the prenatal experience without realizing medical science has never explained it.

When talking with other mothers, Elizabeth learned most women do not realize they have conceived until they notice a missed menstrual period or the physical changes of pregnancy. A first-time mother, she reacted with surprise.

"Doesn't everyone know?" she exclaimed. "I knew I conceived when we made love. So, I began taking care of myself and the baby the first day of my pregnancy."

Paying attention to this intuition was invaluable. *It encouraged her to take care of herself before medical tests could detect what she already knew: a baby was growing within.*

Donna-Lynne, a mother of a boy and a girl living in Baton Rouge, Louisiana, reports: "I've always had, for lack of a better term, paranormal experiences," she recalls. "During pregnancy, they were much more frequent. At the time, I took my experiences for granted. I have never been pregnant before. Yet I always assumed that knowing the time of conception was a feeling all mothers got, and I didn't realize it was unusual until I talked with other people."

Timothy was conceived when Donna-Lynne was still nursing her daughter, Stephanie. She had not yet resumed menstruating after giving birth and had no reason to suspect pregnancy.

After an ultrasound scan, her doctor gave her a February due date. "No," Donna-Lynne insisted, "I conceived my baby on April 24. About a week or so afterward, I felt another presence. Recalculating my due date brought it to January 16. This is the day I gave birth to Timothy."

Other intuitions about the baby frequently accompany the conception intuition. For example, Jan, a mother of four, sensed when her first child was conceived. At the onset of her second pregnancy, she had a similar experience but this time accompanied by a clear intuition of her baby's gender.

"An hour after lovemaking," Jan recalls, "I had the first thoughts we would have a baby, and by the next morning I was sure I had conceived. It was a feeling of fullness, a sense of completion that spilled over into excitement and well-being. I wanted a baby and knew it was happening!

"I visited a friend the next day and told her to remember February 14, 1980, because that was when my baby was conceived. Carl was born November 16, 1980."

"I didn't know the time of conception with my second child, but I was sure I was going to have a son. From the first time I thought of the baby after I realized I was pregnant it was always a boy. After finding out I was pregnant I was thinking I could finally use Carl's clothes again for Paul."

How does the conception intuition occur? Surely no mother can feel sperm and egg uniting. It would be like feeling a single cell in the body. And even if the mother could feel a process so subtle—yet so gigantic in its implications—no expectant father can feel what is happening in his mate's body. Or can he? What is behind the conception intuition? Does the baby somehow announce his or her intention to come into physical existence? Do the parents have a built-in sense that pregnancy has occurred. If they do, why? Is it so they can start taking care of their health, their diet, and their unborn child from the baby's earliest beginnings? Do the parents have an inexplicable means of knowing so subtle that it can match even the most advanced scientific tests? Or is it all just imagination? Wishful thinking?

SUBLIMINAL KNOWLEDGE

We can sometimes explain the conception intuition in terms of the mother's subliminal or even conscious perception of her ovulatory changes. Many women can feel when ovulation occurs. For some it is a pinching sensation. Others notice physical changes such as thickened cervical mucus. Some just "sense" ovulation has occurred without really knowing what is behind this knowledge.

The mother senses she is ovulating while making love. Violà! A conception intuition.

This may sometimes be an explanation for the feeling that a child is conceived. However, Donald Creevy, M.D., assistant professor of obstetrics at Stanford University in California, puts it this way: "There is a big difference between thinking, wondering, fearing, or wishing you were pregnant and having a genuine intuition of conception."

Occasionally, when the conception intuition occurs immediately after lovemaking, it may simply be the result of a woman having paid close attention to her fertile periods. Of course, the probability of conception is high at those times. A woman could easily guess she had become pregnant after lovemaking during her fertile period. For these reasons, it is tempting to write off the conception intuition as the mother's subliminal perception of the subtle but real changes that occur when she is ovulating.

Many mothers have reported suddenly realizing they are pregnant. The intuition sometimes comes to the surface with a sudden feeling of "Aha!" For example, Karen, a technical writer in Austin, Texas, and mother of four—two adopted and two biological children—recalls discovering her second pregnancy in a flash of insight. "When my son Sean was only six months old, my mother-in-law took me clothes shopping. She urged me not to get a particular shirt since I was still nursing and wearing shirts that weren't my usual size.

"I told her, 'I won't be nursing forever,' then I realized I was pregnant again! It couldn't have been more than a day or two after conception."

This intuition may have resulted from an unconscious awareness of subtle physical changes that Karen may have just been beginning to experience. In any event, her perception told her something the most sophisticated scientific test could not have revealed at that point.

In a similar vein, Sharon, a mother of two children recalls: "I've always known the following morning in all five pregnancies, three of which didn't go to term. Among other things I would wake up in the morning dizzy and the smell of coffee would make me positively ill, and I'm a serious coffee drinker."

Naturally, almost all women realize they are pregnant sometime between conception and giving birth. A woman who experiences the early signs of pregnancy and accordingly has a pregnancy test is not necessarily responding to intuition. She is reacting to clearly perceived physical changes.

Sometimes, however, the mother perceives the pregnancy even in the face of medical evidence to the contrary. Tricia, a mother of three in New Jersey, had two inconclusive pregnancy tests. Yet she still knew she was pregnant. "I insisted to the doctor that I was pregnant. So, he sent me to a laboratory for a special test that was positive."

Again, this intuition probably resulted from Tricia's perception, subliminal or conscious, of the physical symptoms of early pregnancy. The important point is her intuition proved correct despite pregnancy test results. Therefore, health professionals would benefit their clients by taking the mother's intuition seriously—even if it initially seems inaccurate.

Subliminal impressions, however, hardly explain how a mother or father could sense the baby's gender or state of health at the time of conception. Besides, women ovulate monthly. If a subliminal perception of ovulation were behind the conception intuition, women would be having such intuitions every month. Yet the conception intuition occurs only rarely.

Lana, a mother in Oregon and software engineer, had an inner sense of being pregnant that cannot be explained in terms of perceiving subliminal physical changes. She recalls, "My husband, Rick, and I have been married for thirteen years and had never tried to conceive until this year. Then we decided to have a child. Immediately after lovemaking on February 6, 1993, I told Rick I was sure I was pregnant."

Her intuition proved true.

There was no chance pregnancy had occurred later. As Lana recalls, "After a death in the family that required three trips across the country, we did not attempt one for many months."

Another mother, Diana, of West Virginia, puts it, "There were times when my period was late and I could have been pregnant. But I never *felt* that I had conceived as I felt when conception occurred. There is a difference in the feeling."

AN INEXPLICABLE FEELING

What distinguishes the conception intuition from the mere thought, wish, or fear that pregnancy has occurred?

In most episodes, conception intuitions have similar distinguishing characteristics. Most occur during, immediately after, or within a few hours of intercourse. The instantaneous knowledge of conception is sometimes difficult, if not impossible, to convey in words. The mother knows. Or the father knows. Occasionally, both parents suddenly realize a child has been conceived.

Many parents find it hard to explain the feeling associated with conception intuitions. Some describe it as a sense of "I know but I don't know how I know." Others describe it as "spiritual," "magical," a "warm, inner glow." Patrick said he felt the creative forces merging. Wendy called it a "distinct realization." Jan depicted it as "a feeling of fullness, a sense of completion." And another mother portrayed it as something with much power and a "special feeling."

WHAT DISTINGUISHES INTUITION FROM A GUESS?

Both men and women may sense a child has been conceived long before medical tests can confirm pregnancy. Here are some hallmarks of this intuition:

- Most occur during or very shortly after lovemaking
- A unique feeling, such as a warm inner glow, a sense of fulfillment, a sense of something spiritual, magical, or otherwise extraordinary
- An inexplicable feeling of knowing ("I know but I don't know how I know")
- The sense of a "third presence"

More often than not, however, conception intuitions are quite undramatic. The intuition is often just below the threshold of consciousness and only announces itself when something like taking a contraceptive pill triggers the thought of pregnancy. Alexis, a Rhode Island psychology major planning to pursue parapsychology, experienced an accidental pregnancy.

"Immediately after lovemaking," Alexis recalls, "I began talking about pregnancy. Hours later, I knew why I had been talking and thinking about pregnancy. I had conceived a child. Two weeks later, I had a positive pregnancy test." Intuition is a common occurrence for Alexis. She frequently knows the gender of a friend's child. "Once while talking with a pregnant friend, I told her I thought she was pregnant with twins, both boys." The intuition, verified months later, was accurate.

During her pregnancy, Alexis, like many mothers, found her intuitive ability magnified. "I was not only more attuned to my own inner feelings but also more connected with my partner," she recalls. "I could sense where he was during the day. Once, after unsuccessfully trying to reach him at home, on a whim, I phoned a local pizza shop where he rarely visits. He was at the restaurant."

For some parents, the intuition occurs in a dream. According to Canadian psychologist Andrew Feldmar, "Women who have learned to pay attention to their dreams can often pinpoint the time they conceived from the unmistakable contents of a dream that occurred no more than a few hours after coitus. The news travels fast."[1]

Occasionally, the feeling accompanying the intuition is unique to the particular parent. For example, Diana knew she had conceived immediately after making love. For Diana, the distinguishing feature of her intuition was quite original. She recalls the feeling accompanying the intuition: "It was almost the same sensation as the quickening. I was utterly sure, although it was not supposed to be the right time to conceive, that we had just made a baby."

Sometimes, one or both parents perceive the conception intuition as a presence of a third party: supposedly the child. This was the experience of Leah, a doctorate student of English at The University of Southwestern Louisiana.

"I knew the instant I conceived my son," Leah recalls. "It is really hard to explain what I felt or saw. In one moment, I just knew. Strangely I perceived the presence as female (but then later in the pregnancy I began to perceive the presence as male). The next day I started looking at maternity clothes. I was a high school teacher at the time and I asked the school nurse if I could be pregnant.

"The nurse said there was no way for me to know that early and that it was the wrong part of my cycle for me to conceive. A fellow teacher who had graduated from medical school told me the same thing. However, I was positive and had a pregnancy test. Sure enough, I was pregnant!"

Some cultures interpret sensing a third party's presence as a message from the spirit of a reincarnating entity.

For example, in one episode reported by anthropologist Antonia Mills, while doing research among the Beaver Indians of British Columbia the expectant father and the mother's brother both knew a pregnancy had occurred. The young father felt someone touch his foot. He was certain it was the ghost of a young woman who had been murdered. "Shortly after this," writes Dr. Mills, "his brother-in-law heard a baby crying in the house. When he went to see whose baby it was, there was no baby."[2]

No baby yet. However, Rita, his brother's wife, had just become pregnant.

THE IMPOSSIBLE THING ABOUT CONCEPTION

The conception intuition occurs to hundreds of mothers and hundreds of fathers. Every day. Common as the phenomenon is, however, there is something extraordinary about it.

Everything we know about biology, pregnancy, and the process of reproduction suggests that realizing conception has occurred during or immediately after lovemaking is completely impossible.

Why impossible? At the time the intuition usually occurs (within minutes of lovemaking), sperm and egg have *not united*. If we define conception—as does medicine and biology—as the union of sperm and egg, we are left with an enigma. For a child is not conceived until several hours after intercourse. Is it possible that we need to redefine conception? To borrow an expression from one expectant father who felt a child as conceived during lovemaking, do the creative forces merge to form a child even before sperm and egg have united?

However, we look at it, some part of the expectant parent's mind seems to know pregnancy has occurred *before it has*.

CHAPTER 2

Do Expectant Mothers Have ESP?

Adrienne, a first-time mother who lives in a suburb of New York City, had an unusual experience during her pregnancy. From conception to birth, she had felt an intuitive connection with her unborn twins and, by some inexplicable means of knowing, sensed that both were girls. However, the experience she had on a night close to her twins' birth was unlike any other.

She woke from a harrowing dream, the most unforgettable dream of her life. "I dreamed that both my girls were developing in the same sac yet had one placenta," Adrienne recalls. Later, an ultrasound confirmed this. Such a detailed description is nothing short of fantastic, since twins can have separate placentas and develop in separate amniotic sacs.

But that was only part of the dream. "I dreamed my unborn girls were crying out to me. They were telling me they had to be born immediately. A few days later, I went into premature labor." Adrienne's physician responded as most physicians would. Without hesitation, he prescribed tocolytic drugs—in other words, medication to stop labor. Yet Adrienne felt her intuition so strongly she refused.

Failure to give tocolytic drugs might very well cause the death of the twins. In addition, the physician had to protect himself from a future malpractice suit. Adrienne refused tocolysis in no uncertain terms. Her physician made her sign a release that she was making a choice against medical advice—a choice that would very likely cost both her children's lives.

Adrienne says, "There was no question—not even a doubt that my children had to be born immediately."

The thoroughly perplexed physician visited Adrienne a few hours after the premature birth. He had just discovered something he'll no doubt remember the rest of his life. Adrienne's twins were severely anemic. In addition, they were suffering an extremely rare disease known as twin-to-twin transfusion syndrome resulting in progressive blood loss.

"I don't know how you knew," the physician told Adrienne. "But had we stopped your labor, you would have lost your beautiful baby girls."

Whether we call it instinct, an inner sense, gut feeling, a propensity for hunches, or just an unaccountable way of knowing, the expectant mother's intuition is legendary. It has guided health professionals. It has announced conceptions, named babies, planned births, inspired dramatic life changes, and saved lives.

Mother's intuition. It's as variable as New England weather. And as unpredictable. Yet so common that just about every pregnant woman who takes a close look within will find it.

Intuition during the prenatal months encompasses a wide range of experiences. These include the following:

- Knowledge that conception has occurred before the physical symptoms of pregnancy appear
- Intuitive dreaming
- The well-documented but baffling father's experience of prenatal symptoms
- A sense of communication with the unborn child
- Lifesaving flashes about medical complications undetected by tests and technology

Mother's intuition may sometimes reflect her body's needs. For example, many believe that pregnancy's legendary food cravings stem from intuition. The craving for unusual and sometimes anything but appetizing substances may reflect the mother's inner knowledge of a substance her body needs (salt, calcium, even trace minerals). Supposedly, her body gives her a message about something that will benefit her or her unborn child—though it is anybody's guess what is behind a craving to eat some of the stranger substances pregnant women have ingested, including inner tubes and lumps of clay!

Admit it nor not, every person has probably had intuitive experiences. Most of these, however, are quite undramatic and often go unnoticed. Who has not thought of Aunt Alice, a relative who has not entered your mind in months? Seconds later the phone rings and there she is on the other end of the line. Is it really coincidence? Probably not. More likely, the experience is a form of intuition.

Are such experiences more common during pregnancy? Are expectant mothers more "psychic" than other people? Do pregnant women have an unaccountable means of knowing? Does the unborn child respond to the mother's thoughts and feelings? The experiences of thousands of parents suggest that the answer to all these questions is yes.

WHAT IS INTUITION?

Intuition is *knowing without the conscious use of reason*. Experts in the field of intuition development have different ideas and definitions of intuition. However, most feel that intuition and reasoning or logical thought are entirely different modes of knowledge with major distinctions between them.

A great gulf separates the commonsense world of rational thinking and the unruly realm of intuition. Rational knowledge is slow, plodding, and always based on our knowledge and experience. Intuition, on the other hand, is immediate and is not limited to what we know or have experienced.

Or to put it another way, intuition extends beyond ourselves, unlike the rational mind. The rational part of ourself is limited, finite. Intuition, by distinction, transcends space, time, and is almost unlimited, infinite in its scope. What other way can we explain knowing something before it happens? Or sensing someone across the nation is dialing our phone at the very minute she is?

Despite the great difference between the two, intuition and rational thinking can work in harmony. In the attempt to make intuition seem less mysterious, some have tried to define intuition as a species of logic. For example, Laurence Sprecher of Public Management Associates in Oregon suggests that intuition is logical thinking hidden in the subconscious portion of the brain. "If we accepted that intuition is an extension of the logical, wouldn't we be more comfortable using it? By treating intuition as something mysterious or, worse yet, feminine, do we not make it more difficult for most managers, who tend to be biologically masculine and theoretically logical, to use intuition?"[1]

Calling intuition "feminine" implies it is primarily a woman's experience and the often-heard term *women's intuition*, conveys the idea that intuition is more common in women than in men. There are two reasons for this. First, women tend to be more in touch with their feelings and are likely to be aware of intuitive experiences everyone may have. Second, it is culturally acceptable for females to pay attention to and discuss their instinctual feelings and "gut reactions." Accordingly, women may be less likely to dismiss intuitive experiences as irrational or unscientific.

In real life, however, intuition is not gender-specific. Research studies show little or no difference in intuitive ability between males and females. For instance, extensive collections of intuitive experiences made by the British Society of Psychical Research show that episodes of intuition are equally divided between the sexes. Fifty-eight percent were reported by women and 42 percent were reported by men.[2] In another extensive study of intuition among schoolchildren in Uttar Pradesh, India, Ian Stevenson, M.D., professor of psychiatry at the University of Virginia Medical School, found an almost equal number of boys and girls reported intuitive occurrences.[3]

THE EXPLAINED AND THE UNEXPLAINED

We can divide intuitive experiences roughly into two broad categories: *explicable* and *inexplicable*.

Explicable intuition is based on what we know, the contents of our mind and the results of our experience. We can explain these intuitive experiences in terms of psychology, medicine, and other forms of conventional science. More often than not, *explicable* intuition reflects subliminal impressions, heightened awareness of the body, and increased sensitivity both to the external environment and to inner feelings.

Inexplicable intuition, on the other hand, transcends our personal knowledge and experience. We cannot explain this form of intuitive experience in terms of anything that conventional science, medicine, or psychology know about the body or mind.

Parapsychologists, scientists who investigate instances of telepathy, clairvoyance, and other "psychic" phenomena, classify this type of intuition as *paranormal*. *Webster's* defines *paranormal* as "not scientifically explainable; supernatural."

Psi is the abbreviated term for all psychic phenomena, including the categories of extrasensory perception discussed ahead. By whatever name, inexplicable intuition remains an inexplicable means of knowing.

Psi—far from extraordinary and exceptional as most people believe—may be a characteristic of all life. For example, some telepathic ordering principle may be behind the intricate flight patterns of migrating birds. Evidence of psi is found throughout the natural world. Cleve Backster, a former CIA agent turned parapsychologist, showed that plants react to the death of nearby brine shrimp.[4]

Since the nineteenth century, researchers associated with the Society for Psychical Research in Great Britain and the American Society for Psychical Research in New York City have studied parapsychological phenomena. However, Dr. J. B. Rhine pioneered the first definitive American study of intuition at Duke University in Raleigh, North Carolina, in the 1930s.

Rhine, who is known as the "father of experimental parapsychology," called this unexplained means of knowing *extrasensory perception*. Today, the technical term for inexplicable intuition is still *extrasensory perception* or, more commonly, *ESP*.

Dr. Rhine experimented with ESP at Duke University. In one course of experiments (known as the Pearce-Pratt series), Zener cards were used. Developed by psychologist Dr. Karl Zener, Zener cards consist of a pack of twenty-five cards, five each of five geometric figures: a star, a circle, a cross, a wavy line, and a rectangle. Testing relied on a simple principle. One person called an *agent* would concentrate on a symbol while another person called a *subject* would "guess" the symbol.

During the Pearce-Pratt series, subject and agent were in two different buildings more than 100 yards apart. Of a total of 1,850 "guesses," 558 responses proved correct. Chance would account for only 370 correct hits. The number of correct guesses was so much greater than this that the odds of this occurring by mere guessing were twenty-two thousand million to one.[5]

In one extraordinary ESP test done at Harvard University, in 1925–26, researcher George Estabrooks used standard playing cards, separating subjects and experimenters in a double room by a door. When the subject was to guess the card the experimenter held, a red light flashed. They made 83 different sets of 20 guesses totaling 1,600 guesses. The results were more than 100 correct guesses above the

TYPES OF ESP

Four common forms of estrasensory perception occur in daily life and are especially common during the childbearing year.
These are as follows:

- *Telepathy:* communication from one mind to another through channels other than our five senses
- *Clairvoyance:* the experience of discerning objects or situations not present to the senses
- *Precognition:* clairvoyance about an event or condition that hasn't yet occurred
- *Telesomatic symptoms:* the experience of feeling in one's own body the physical symptoms of another

chance level. The odds of this happening by sheer chance were ten million to one.[6]

Synchronicity, a term coined by world-renowned psychologist Carl Jung, is another word for inexplicable coincidences. Jung defines this phenomenon with the rather impenetrable sentence: "Synchronicity takes the coincidence of events in space and time as meaning something more than mere chance, namely, a peculiar interdependence of objective events among themselves as well as with the subjective (psychic) states of the observer or observers."[7] This means that there is no known cause for certain events that seem to take place simultaneously and appear more than coincidence. Thinking of an old friend just before passing him or her on the street may be an example of either telepathy or synchronicity.

Documented laboratory evidence is essential to provide a background for parapsychology as a science. However it does not capture the flavor of intuition in real life any more than studying embryology captures the feeling of being pregnant. As psychiatrist and parapsychological researcher Jan Ehrenwald, M.D., points out in his *ESP Experience: A Psychiatric Validation,* "The proving ground is not the experimental laboratory; it is life in the raw: the parent-child relationship, the family situation, clinic and consulting room, and human affairs in general."[8]

Many agree with this commonsense view. In 1962, *The International Journal of Parapsychology* surveyed many astute scholars with an interest in parapsychological studies. These included Carl Jung; Ian Stevenson, professor of psychiatry at the University of Virginia; J. B. Rhine of Duke University; and several others. All agreed that insight about intuition required real-life stories.

IN SEARCH OF THE UNEXPLAINED

Despite the tremendous difference between explicable and inexplicable intuition, it is difficult, and sometimes impossible, to distinguish the two from one another.

Experiences that first appear to be be ESP may, on a closer look, prove explicable in other ways. For example, one mother reports: "I had an inescapable sense that something was wrong during my second pregnancy. I told my physician about my worry but he just assured me there was no cause for concern. The baby was fine. My apprehension lingered until finally I was admitted to the hospital in premature labor. The baby had to be taken to an intensive care nursery because of the premature birth."

While this event may be ESP, there is another possibility. The mother, who had been pregnant before, may have perceived just beneath the threshold of consciousness a difference in fetal activity between this and her former pregnancy. This subliminal impression of less fetal movement could register as the feeling that something was wrong.

Many intuitive experiences result from subliminal impressions like this. For example, a mother's labor stops progressing. Initially she may not realize the cause. However, she turns inward and asks herself why this is occurring. She may suddenly realize that she is holding her labor back because of intense mixed feelings regarding becoming a mother and continuing her career. The intuition reflects the mother's own feelings that may not have been conscious until she examined them.

Many other intuition cases, however, are not the result of subliminal perceptions. For example, one expectant mother reported: "For the first time in years, I thought of an old college friend. Minutes later she telephoned. I would often think of someone while out shopping only to find a message from that person on my answering machine when I returned. Though I never had these experiences before, they happened quite frequently throughout my pregnancy."

COMMON INTUITIVE OCCURRENCES DURING PREGNANCY

- A sudden thought that seems to reveal information beyond the senses
- Flashes of insight following working on a problem
- Emotions, usually coming as a feeling "out of the blue," often concerning another who is at that moment experiencing a crisis

Experts in parapsychology frequently use a general rule of thumb when examining probable ESP reports. To qualify as ESP, the episode cannot be explained *in any other way*. This guideline has both benefit and disadvantage. The benefit is insuring reported ESP cases are paranormal. The disadvantage is that many events that may be genuine ESP are ruled out because they might be explicable in terms of subliminal impressions.

Though validating ESP and distinguishing it from explicable intuition is only important in the field of parapsychology, both types of intuition can play a valuable role in daily life. During pregnancy, giving more attention to intuition may lead to better maternal-child health and open the door on a fascinating yet unexplored dimension of the creation of life. Whether one has ever been an expectant parent, appreciating intuition can give us a richer perception of life itself.

THE MANY FACES OF INTUITION

People experience intuition as thoughts, sudden insights, emotions, and even physical symptoms.[9] In whatever form—as thought, emotion, or physical sensation—intuition rarely announces herself with high drama. Though occasional intuitive experiences wake some people from a sound sleep, these are the exceptional episodes. Unlike the dramatic never-to-be forgotten ESP experiences that are the staple of certain TV shows, most episodes are subtle and undramatic. Frequently a flash of intuition fleets across the corner of your mind like a half-remembered dream. Many people find that it takes deliberate effort and practice to notice the intuitive voice.

Intuition, particularly the solution to a difficult problem, may come as a feeling of well-being, a sense of sudden insight, or in the words of top-ranking executives, "a sense of excitement—almost euphoria," "growing excitement in the pit of [one's] stomach," "a total sense of commitment," "a feeling of complete harmony," and "a bolt of lightning or sudden flash that this is the solution."[10]

How the inner voice appears probably depends on a combination of personality and beliefs. A spiritually oriented person is likely to experience the intuitive voice during prayer. Someone who practices yoga may have flashes of insight during meditation. A skilled psychic may perceive complex details instantaneously. Yet others have a variety of intuitive experiences that do not seem to follow any particular pattern.

Paying greater attention to intuition may lead to an increase in intuitive experiences. Acting on a sudden urge to phone someone who pops into mind for no apparent reason is one way to expand awareness of intuition. You may discover that the person was trying to contact you! Validating such experiences can develop greater confidence in "gut feelings." (Practical methods for developing your own intuition are included in chapter 10, "Developing Your Intuition.")

Learning to pay attention to the body's subtle (and sometimes not so subtle) messages and linking them to intuition when appropriate is yet another way to expand intuitive awareness.

THE NATURE OF INTUITION

Dr. Charles Tart, psychology professor at the University of California at Davis, believes that ESP is a very involved psychological process, analogous in complexity to dreaming. Intuitive information seems to flow into the unconscious mind and changes because of personality and unconscious dynamics.[11]

As parapsychological writer D. Scott Rogo puts it: "ESP functions in two stages—the subconscious first assembles the ESP data and then transfers them to conscious awareness. There are many ways the gap between the conscious and unconscious can be bridged—dreams, intuitions, impressions, hallucinations, and so forth—and it is just in these ways that most ESP manifests in daily life."[12]

Without consciously planning it that way, some people seem to "specialize" in particular topics, for example, predicting an unborn child's gender, intuiting complications of pregnancy, and so on. Dr. Stevenson says, "Cultural races or attitudes of a people may influence the paranormal as well as the normal feature of these experiences."[13] Also, one's personality may influence the subjects about which he or she is intuitive.

Intuition sometimes accompanies a feeling one should follow rather than ignore the subtle voice within. It is especially important to pay attention to such feelings when reviewing important decisions such as the choice of a birth environment or health care provider.

Ignoring intuition often accompanies an unpleasant nettling feeling that one is not behaving in the optimal way. According to Professor Weston Agor, director of the Master in Public Administration Program at the University of Texas at El Paso, executives who rely on their intuition "also seemed to share a common set of feelings when they sensed an impending decision was inappropriate or that they needed to take more time to adequately process the cues they were receiving to arrive at the best decision possible. At these times, managers speak of 'a sense of anxiety,' 'mixed signals,' 'discomfort,' 'sleepless nights,' or an 'upset stomach.' "[14]

The inner voice is often characterized by a sense of immediacy. The knowledge often appears "out of the blue." One psychologist expressed it this way. "If you don't know how you know something, it's probably intuition."

THE ESP OF PREGNANCY

Parents experience a variety of intuitive experiences during pregnancy. Among these are conception intuitions, gender intuitions, flashes of insight about the baby's characteristics or possibly developing problems, feelings of communication with the unborn child, frequent experiences of telepathy between mother and father, and even physical symptoms of pregnancy in a family member other than the mother-to-be. (Physical ESP, called *telesomatic symptoms,* is discussed in chapter 4.)

Second to conception intuition, gender intuition is probably the most common form of pregnancy intuition. It is sometimes clear and distinct and sometimes a vague "sixth" sense. Thousands of parents experience it, some without even realizing that what they are experiencing is beyond the realm of ordinary knowledge.

As Cathy, a mother of three, recalls, "My firstborn was a son, and I don't know how I knew, but I always felt he was a boy child."

COMMON PREGNANCY INTUITIONS

The following common pregnancy intuitions may appear as a thought, emotion, sudden flash of insight, dream, or physical sensation:

- *The conception intuition*—knowledge that a child has been conceived before medical tests can confirm conception
- *Gender intuition*—knowledge of the unborn child's gender
- *Intuitions about the baby*—knowledge of the baby's physical characteristics or even of developing complications
- *Labor intuitions*—intuitions that labor is about to begin (called the *nesting instinct*) or will begin at some specific future time
- *Telepathy between the mother and other family members*
- *Couvade symptoms*—the experience of pregnancy symptoms in the father, relative, or close friend of the mother

A similar intuitive feeling occurred during Cathy's second pregnancy. "I *knew* I was carrying a girl. It's hard to explain, maybe I felt feminine or something, but I never had any question in my mind about carrying a girl."

Renée, a mother of two in San Francisco, chose her children's names on the strength of her intuition. "I somehow knew my first two kids' gender," she recalls. "I even made a Christmas stocking for my first with girl colors and her name. With my second I wanted another girl but I knew it was going to be a boy. We never did pick girl names."

Dona, a mother and computer programmer living in Ann Arbor, Michigan, experienced a similar gender intuition. She reports, "I knew the baby was a girl. I couldn't even fathom the possibility of having a boy. We tried to get an ultrasound to verify gender and had several ultrasound scans because of pregnancy complications. None confirmed my intuition. Our child is a girl."

Intuiting the child's gender goes along with intuiting other facts about the unborn baby. For example, Marryn, a mother and graphic designer from Seattle, Washington, had no doubt that her unborn child was a girl. "Halfway through the first trimester," Marryn recalls, "I realized I was referring to my child as 'she.' "

By the second trimester she knew her baby girl was going to be healthy. There would not be anything remarkable about this if she had not previously experienced two tragic miscarriages, each preceded by an intuition the baby would die.

Nancy, a Virginia mother of two girls and a boy, recalls knowing the gender of her children early in pregnancy. "With our first child, David, my husband and I chose only boys' names and we bought blue clothes. I just knew he was a boy and he was."

"I also knew our second child, Stefanie, was a petite girl. I don't have a clue why, but for some reason our obstetrician got the idea in his head our child was going to be a boy. I think it had something to do with the heartbeat or one of those other old wive's tales."

Though I kept telling him my baby would be a small girl, he wanted to do an ultrasound scan. "I don't want to have the test because I am not into unnecessary medical intervention," I told him. "But I finally had the ultrasound during the last month of pregnancy. And sure enough the baby was a petite girl."

Nancy continued to feel an extrasensory connection as her children grew. "When Stefanie moved into her own room, I used to reach out to her with my mind just to be sure she was okay. One night, I felt there was nothing there. I sat up in a panic. Stefanie was not in her bed, I could feel it. I asked my husband to check on her. He got out of bed and found that Stefanie had wandered into her brother's room."

Many expectant mothers take their intuition for granted and do not realize that the episode they consider commonplace is inexplicable in terms of anything but parapsychology.

Sally, the natural mother of two, and stepmother of six, feels there is nothing remarkable about knowing the child's gender. "I think most women know the gender of the child they are carrying," she says. "They have a sixth sense about it."

During her first pregnancy with Richard, her sixth sense about her child's gender influenced both her postpartum preparations and her own behavior during pregnancy. "I had the feeling of masculinity," she recalls. "Throughout the pregnancy, it was as if my entire being were more masculine. I wore jeans, T-shirts, and other 'boy' clothing. Because of my masculine interests, my husband bought me a motorcycle—hardly a typical gift for a pregnant woman—and we took motor-cycle trips. After Richard was born, we sold it!

"When I had a baby shower, many people gave me girl's pink clothing. I asked for the names of the stores where they bought the clothing so I could exchange it. I knew the child was going to be a boy."

Sally had a similar "gut feeling" during her second pregnancy with her daughter Melissa. "During the pregnancy, I tended to wear more frilly clothes and laces because I felt 'girl.' One thing I bought was a bassinet I lined with satin and decorated with lace and ribbons. I bought dozens of girl's dresses. It would have been a [wardrobe] disaster had Melissa been a boy!"

Sally is not the only one who selected baby clothing on the strength of her intuition. Danielle had a similar experience. "My daughter was born a few days before Christmas in 1987," recalls Danielle. "From the beginning of my pregnancy I was absolutely sure this baby was going to be a girl. I saw mental pictures of her, with her cute turned-up button nose and brown curly hair."

Nothing that we know about the physiology of pregnancy explains or even suggests how a mother can intuit the gender of her unborn child. Yet even expectant fathers and other family members and friends have such intuitions about the unborn baby.

Is the parents' feeling about the unborn child's gender always correct?

Despite many remarkable case histories, the feeling that a child may be a boy or girl is often wrong—as many parents have discovered. This makes it particularly difficult to distinguish intuition—that is, certain knowledge without the conscious use of reason—and sheer guesswork.

As Ed, a Connecticut father, recalls, "When my wife was pregnant, everyone knew our child was a girl. People stopped her on the street and said, 'Looks like a girl' or 'You're carrying the baby like a girl.' People who purported psychic ability confirmed this and proclaimed, 'Girl!'

"In the birthing room I caught the baby," Ed continues. "The midwife said, 'Tell the mommy what it is!'

"I was confused. 'Its a baby!' Then I realized, 'Oh, you mean the sex!' "

"We named him Stephen."

More often than not, there is no way of verifying whether the gender intuition was an actual intuition or a guess. For example, James, a man from South Carolina, recalls, "My best friends are recent parents with a two year old and a newborn. In both cases I felt I knew the sex of the child almost as soon as I was aware of the pregnancy, and both times I was right. It was no 'lucky guess'; I felt certain that I knew and I was correct."

While this experience may very well have been extrasensory, there is really no way of telling. Occasionally, intuition revealing information about the unborn child surfaces as a vague feeling or almost as something one knows but has forgotten.

For example, Alexis's second pregnancy ended in a miscarriage. "About a month into the pregnancy, I knew something was not right. It just didn't feel healthy. A month or so after that, I miscarried."

As often as not, two or more intuitions go hand in hand. For example, a parent may intuit conception, the gender of the child, and perhaps other facts simultaneously.

Gerry, a computer programmer and father of two living children and one stillborn, experienced gender intuitions almost immediately after conception with all three of his children. His intuition occurs on what he calls a "reaction basis." As he puts it, "I'm only hit with the realization that I know the information when someone asks." In all three cases of Gerry's gender intuition, he knew the gender when his wife asked him for his feelings on the subject.

"Our first was a boy and I knew he would be healthy," recalls Gerry. "Our second was a girl and I knew she would not survive. This turned out to be true. Our third came after two years of trying and I knew he would be a boy."

Often, the source of intuition remains a mystery.

For instance, Jack, a father of two, shares a tragic intuition his wife experienced.

"After eight and a half years of trying to have children and giving up all hope," Jack recalls, "my wife told me that she felt she was pregnant. She told me this only a few minutes after we made love. About a month later we discovered that she was pregnant. She gave birth to a boy.

"A year and half later, she gave birth to our daughter. Shortly after our daughter was born she told me that she felt that she wouldn't live to raise our children. When our daughter was seventeen months old, my wife died in an automobile accident. It has really been tough, especially since I have become an incomplete quadriplegic since my wife's death. But I still have my children and I love them very much.

"Now they both are my arms and legs. Now that my son just turned fourteen and my daughter twelve and a half, I often think of these things and wonder how she could have known."

Vanessa, a department store manager in Birmingham, Alabama, knew without question that she had conceived on Valentine's Day. "I chalk it up to women's intuition," she says. "There was so much power and such a special feeling."

She also knew her child was a girl. "It's really hard to explain but I just felt 'this has got to be a girl!'"

Tragically, she also knew her baby would not live to full term. Vanessa experienced bleeding early during pregnancy and had to remain on bed rest throughout the following months. At five and a half months, she went into labor. "Finally, I felt a peace and sense of relief. They told me there was still a chance. But I knew she was gone.

"I want people to know that suffering a loss doesn't mean you have to quit," says Vanessa. She is now pregnant again. "I wanted a little girl, mainly because of the death of my daughter, but I know in my heart it's a boy. Healthy and kicking. And I'm really excited!"

THE TELEPATHIC FAMILY

Though many parents are not consciously aware of it, telepathy between husband and wife is common during pregnancy—even among couples who have never had extrasensory experiences previously.

For example, Roxana experienced an extraordinary series of telepathic dreams about her husband, who was in the military service at the time.

She reports: "I began having vivid dreams about army tactical exercises. With my husband away so much of the time I sent one dream via electronic mail to a friend who was an officer specializing in surface warfare. He was amazed how accurately the dream revealed what were supposed to be secret strategies!

"At the time of the dreams, I thought my husband was just working on a computer. But it turned out he was traveling with special forces on war exercises."

During pregnancy, intuitive experiences are more common among the entire family and sometimes close friends.

For example, Susan, an assistant professor in Maine, recalls how her son Christopher, a three-and-a-half-year-old boy, appeared to intuit her second pregnancy and even the unborn child's gender before she knew she was pregnant.

"I had no inkling whatsoever that I was pregnant until probably one and a half months into the pregnancy," says Susan.

"A couple of weeks before I learned I was pregnant, Chris asked me in the car on the way home one day how he could get a brother or a sister. My husband and I had never discussed having another baby with him and had not even really talked about it between ourselves where he could have overheard anything. I told Chris that I would have to have a baby.

" 'You mean you'd have a baby in your belly?' he asked.

" 'Yes,' I told him.

"He dropped the conversation until a few days later. Again he asked me how he could get a baby brother or sister and I gave him the same answer.

" 'I think you do have a baby in your tummy,' he said.

" 'What do you mean?' I asked him.

" 'I think you have a baby in your tummy right now.' I asked him what made him think that. He said he just knew it. Later, I repeated this conversation to my husband with a chuckle.

"However, two weeks afterward, I looked back on this conversation with amazement when I realized that I really was pregnant. We told Chris the news. He talked about how happy he was to be having a little sister. We explained that it might be a little brother. But he was sure it would be a girl. At birth we discovered Chris was right. He did indeed get his little sister!"

Intuitive episodes like this often occur even when the person experiencing the intuition lives a distance from the expectant mother. When she was pregnant with her second child, Sally experienced an intuition so forceful that it woke her in the very early morning.

"My stepdaughter Dawn was pregnant just when I was, our babies being born three months apart. I hadn't spoken to her in a couple of years and didn't even realize she was pregnant. However, one night I woke from a vivid dream about her and felt as though I had to call. At 4:30 A.M., I felt I shouldn't hold back from calling. She picked up the phone on the first ring. She had been awake and was feeling apprehensive about a cesarean scheduled for that morning. She wanted to call me but didn't want to disturb me at that hour."

When a pregnancy occurs, Sheryl, a nurse in Michigan, finds her entire family experiencing telepathic episodes, particularly when something is wrong. "We always seem to have a feeling when something goes wrong with someone in the family and know to call that person," she relates.

Many parents experience intuition during pregnancy and the weeks following and do not feel especially intuitive before or after pregnancy. For example, Marryn felt she had an extrasensory link with her newborn daughter, Colleen, and frequently woke just before her daughter began stirring.

Within a couple of weeks of giving birth, Marryn found her intuitive experiences dwindled away. "After Colleen was born," she recalls, "I felt shut down, as if someone had turned off the juice."

For other parents, intuitive experiences frequently continue into the baby's infancy, if not throughout their lives. What can we conclude about the wide variety of intuitive events occurring to expectant parents? Pregnancy, it seems, is a peak period for intuition. Participating in the miracle of creating life may make the expectant mother privy to an awareness beyond the personal self. For that matter, it almost seems as if she is connected to all life and the universe itself.

CHAPTER 3

The Metamorphosis of Pregnancy

Perhaps below the surface of our awareness we are all connected. Mysterious as it appears, the paranormal may be a characteristic of all living things from plants to people. Everyone may have an extrasensory link with family, with friends, and with the very universe. However, the expectant mother, who is creating new life, may be closer to this connection.

Pregnancy. It is perhaps nature's greatest mystery—as awesome as the creation of the earth. Yet, since it occurs every day all around us, we sometimes overlook how magical it is. Compared to what occurs when the baby transforms herself from a tadpole to the person who looks a little like grandma, intuition seems small business. The incredible is written into the very nature of pregnancy.

It would take a philosopher to find the beauty in morning sickness. But who can fail to feel awe at the miracle of creating new life? From the moment sperm and egg unite in microscopic matrimony, a transformation more magical than a fairy tale occurs. A speck smaller than the dot at the end of this sentence grows to become 200 billion times its original mass. The uterus—baby's private universe—expands to contain a thousand times its original capacity.

Once pregnancy occurs, the mother's entire being changes to adapt to her developing child. While the expectant mother's condition ranges from nauseous and exhausted to glowing and healthy, every organ, every organ system, everything—from her blood to her emotions—undergoes a metamorphosis. And it all begins in the womb.

The metamorphosis of pregnancy seems to radiate outward, like the ever-widening concentric circles made by a stone thrown in a pond, from a single hub: the womb. As pregnancy progresses, the mystery of new life unfolds. From tiny beginnings invisible to the naked eye, pregnancy encompasses the mother's body, her mind, her emotions, and her family.

Throughout the life-creating months, the sexual organs see the most dramatic changes. The uterus, shaped like an inverted pear, expands so much it gently displaces all other abdominal organs, from lungs to liver. Sturdy muscular walls thicken to keep the baby snug and secure in its temporary home.

The *cervix* (neck of the uterus that protrudes into the vagina) softens from a muscular ball hard as the tip of the nose until it is as soft as an earlobe. Simultaneously, the vagina's velvety walls shade from a delicate pink to a rich violet, resulting from an increased blood supply. Meanwhile the vaginal walls become more stretchable and elastic, preparing to open a gateway on the day of birth.

Orchestrated by hormones produced by the developing placenta, the breasts begin to prepare for baby's first feeding. Early in pregnancy, often even before she knows she is pregnant, the mother begins to create baby's only perfect food.

Her skin changes, darkening around the nipples and sometimes becoming pigmented in other areas throughout the body. Even her blood undergoes a transformation, increasing in volume by as much as 40 percent to meet the needs of her changing body and growing child.

Dramatic as they are, the expectant mother's physical transmutations are only part of the metamorphosis of pregnancy. As her body sees a change as amazing as that of caterpillar into butterfly, her mind may be opening a window on the paranormal.

What is behind this legendary intuition? What triggers the pregnant mother's heightened mental power? What gives her the edge on extrasensory awareness? To what does she owe her ESP? After a century of research no one has yet explained ESP. Yet it may be more closely connected to pregnancy than most people realize.

THE "CRADLE OF ESP"

Pregnancy may be the very source of extrasensory perception.

Psychiatrist Jan Ehrenwald, M.D., proposed one of the most unusual theories perhaps ever suggested in the field of psychiatry, parapsychology, and probably any other science. He theorized that the closeness of mother and child—a symbiotic union in the womb—is the root of all psi. Telepathy, clairvoyance, precognition—everything we think of as paranormal—has, according to his theory, one common source: the closeness of mother and child in the womb. Dr. Ehrenwald calls this the *cradle of ESP*.

He defines symbiosis as a "physiological reciprocal dependent relationship between two different organisms, beneficial for both."[1] The mother and child's ego boundaries have not yet separated but are merged into one in the early postpartum period so that "the baby is a direct extension of its mother's body image."[2]

"A telepathic factor may indeed be involved in the early—or even later—child-parent relationship,"[3] he says. Telepathy, in his view, is actually psychic communication within a single, psychological personality while mother and child are still one."[4]

Other scientists, from physicists to psychologists, believe that human infants have a telepathic link with their mothers throughout pregnancy. What purpose does extrasensory perception serve? As Dr. Jonas Salk puts it: "It is not in the nature of nature to provide living organisms with biological tendencies unless such tendencies have survival value."[5]

Do paranormal abilities have survival value?

WHY THE EXPECTANT MOTHER MAY BE MORE INTUITIVE

Pregnancy causes the following changes:

- A life crisis
- A close physical bond with her unborn child
- Introspection
- Greater awareness of the body and subtle sensations
- Greater right brain hemisphere orientation
- Heightened emotional sensitivity
- Greater closeness to unconscious processes such as dreaming
- Greater closeness to the *collective unconscious,* that part of ourselves many psychologists believe is beyond the personal self and linked with all life

---

California obstetrician and pioneer hypnotherapist Dr. David Cheek suggests one possible reason for telepathy between mother and unborn child. He bases his evidence on the psychic experiences of more than a thousand patients. He feels knowledge of maternal thoughts may have survival value for young mammals before they can struggle for themselves without protection.

"After birth," he suggests, "there has to be a total readiness for silent messages from the mother when danger is present. There must be absolute obedience when the mother senses danger."

Pregnancy renders the female mammal vulnerable to predators. She is especially so when labor commences[6] and may intuit the time of labor in advance to get to a safe place. "It seems logical," Dr. Cheek goes on to say that "the communication system is complete prior to birth."[7]

Bear in mind that these ideas are only theories. A more religious person might simply say that ESP was the soul's ability to perceive beyond our physical senses. The fact is we don't know the source of ESP, why it exists, or even what practical value it has.

DAWN OF A NEW MIND

Whether there is anything to Dr. Ehrenwald's cradle of ESP theory, there is little question that, as pregnancy progresses, the mother experiences many psychological and emotional changes that may predispose her to heightened intuition.

The first condition expectant mothers experience that may trigger heightened intuition is pregnancy's life-crisis nature. Many parapsychologists have found that crisis is a primary, if not *the* primary, condition triggering intuitive experiences.

For example, more than a hundred years ago, in 1882, a team of astute investigators joined forces to form the British Society of Psychical Research (SPR). These men included Professor Henry Sidgwick of Cambridge, F. W. H. Myers of Cambridge, the physicist Lord Rayleigh, and other scholars. Their goal: collecting and analyzing well-authenticated psi episodes from thought transference to reports of house hauntings.

With attention to meticulous detail, three SPR researchers—F.W.H. Myers, Frank Podmore, and a skeptically minded lawyer named Edmund Gurney—collected, investigated, verified, and later published hundreds of ESP episodes in a huge volume called *Phantasms of the Living*. The book remains a classic in parapsychological research.

During investigation, the parapsychological researchers stumbled across a recurring phenomenon. Of the hundreds of mind-boggling ESP episodes they investigated, the most unforgettable occurred during times of crisis. For example, Jeanie's lifesaving paranormal vision of her dying mother—one of the most dramatic psychic experiences ever recorded in the annals of psychic science—is an example of what the SPR called *crisis telepathy,* that is, telepathy triggered by an upheaval or major life event.

A ten-year-old girl, Jeanie was walking along a country lane near her home reading a math book, "a subject little likely to produce fancies," she notes. Suddenly, the impossible occurred.

While still alone in the country lane, Jeanie saw a bedroom in her home. "And upon the floor lay my mother," she recalls, "to all appearance dead. The vision must have remained some minutes, during which my real surroundings appeared to pale and die out; but as the vision faded, the actual surroundings came back, at first dimly, and then clearly."

There was no doubt in Jeanie's mind. What she experienced was real. She rushed immediately to the nearby home of her family physician. "He at once set out with me for my home," says Jeanie, "on the way putting questions I could not answer, as my mother to all appearance was well when I left home."

The little girl led the doctor immediately to the bedroom. Her mother was lying there just as she was in the vision. "She had been seized suddenly by an attack at the heart and would soon have breathed her last but for the doctor's timely advent."[8]

By some mechanism of clairvoyance we will probably never fully understand, Jeanie saw on the screen of her mind precisely what her mother was experiencing in another location. Acting on her intuition saved her mother's life. Parapsychologists have found that disaster frequently precipitates experiences of crisis telepathy, though rarely one as dramatic as this.

When pregnancy occurs most mothers- or fathers-to-be hopefully don't experience it as a disaster. But health care professionals agree that pregnancy is a *normal life crisis* if we use the standard defintion of a crisis as the impact of any event that challenges the assumed state of the world and forces the individual to change his view of, or readapt to, the world. During crisis, there is often a period of disequilibrium.[9]

Since childbearing requires great change in family structure, it produces a *developmental* (that is, normal) crisis in the family. Nursing researcher Laurie Sherwen, Ph.D, and former assistant professor at the Graduate Parent-Child Nursing Program at Rutgers University, in New Jersey, points out: "The concept of crisis contains both positive and negative aspects. If handled well, it allows for a higher, more complex level of functioning, through incorporation of new coping strategies."[10]

Every mother's reaction to pregnancy is unique. No one-size-fits-all pattern of thoughts and feelings describes everyone. Many similarities, however, typify the mother-to-be's experience.

When she learns she will soon be crossing the one-way bridge from woman to mother, the expectant mother confronts a period of discovery and adjustment. During the initial prenatal months, she is usually focused on herself, her inner feelings, her changing life.

Once she first begins to feel the baby moving (usually sometime between sixteen and eighteen weeks after conception), her life typically begins to revolve around a new axis: her child. During the final months of pregnancy, she experiences a nesting period, preparing for the day of the birth and her soon-to-be changed role. Her thoughts, emotions, and plans turn to the future child. She prepares her home, usually takes childbirth classes or seeks out some self-education about birth, and finalizes her birth plans. As these changes occur, the expectant mother encounters mixed feelings and emotions so powerful that it may some-times seem she is caught up in something she can't control. As Pamela, a bank loan officer in New Jersey, recalls of the months she was expect-ing her first baby: "At times I felt I wasn't my own person anymore. It was frightening."

Researcher and psychologist Patricia Maybruck, Ph.D., observes that the crisis character of pregnancy may make the parents more prone to heightened intuition, particularly telepathy between expectant mother and father.[11] For example, during her first pregnancy, Marryn, a mother who lives in Seattle, Washington, had many spontaneous episodes of apparent crisis telepathy. Most were associated with her family and her fiancé, Derek.

"During pregnancy, Derek was in training for the special forces in the military," Marryn describes. "Suddenly, a horrible feeling gripped me. I knew something terrible was going to happen. Hysterical with this inexplicable fear, I telephoned the fort where Derek was training and asked about him.

"The bewildered man who answered the phone had no clue why I was practically crying into the phone demanding to know about my fiancé. Everything was fine. Nothing had occurred, the man told me.

"Then, as we were speaking, I heard in the background at the other end of the line someone shouting, 'Emergency!' Our call was abruptly terminated.

"The man later returned my call to tell me Derek had just been caught in an explosion. He was injured. But, thankfully, he wasn't seriously hurt."

This appears to be a clear example of crisis telepathy—an experience of the paranormal. Marryn didn't know her fiancé was involved in army tactical exercises at the time. However, she experienced the sudden dread that something had happened, perhaps at the very minute her fiancé was caught in the explosion.

The second condition that may heighten the mother's intuition is her close physical and emotional bond with her child. The majority of ESP cases parapsychologists have investigated occur between family members: husband and wife, brother and sister, mother and child.

Dr. Ian Stevenson, professor of psychiatry at the University of Virginia, has analyzed hundreds of contemporary cases of probable telepathy and agrees that the majority occur between family members or those with close emotional ties.[12] And who can be closer than mother and unborn child? They breathe the same air, eat the same food. The same blood courses through their veins. To all outward appearances, they even appear to be the same person. And as psychiatrist Dr. Ehrenwald has theorized, they may even think the same thoughts. The strongest of all ties—physiological and emotional—occurs between mother and unborn child. It is not surprising, therefore, that mother and unborn may share telepathic communication.

Nisa, an Australian naturopathic physician and mother of two, feels that the nonphysical connection between her and her unborn children is something as natural as blood flowing through the veins.

"I felt there was an open line of communication between my baby and myself," Nisa says. "It almost felt as though the communication traveled somehow through our bloodstreams.

"During pregnancy, I felt I knew the personalities of both babies before birth, their likes and dislikes in the foods I ate and the music I played.

"With certain foods. I sensed feelings of liking or nausea. The feelings were somehow distant even though I was feeling them. With music, reading, physical intimacy, and so on, I would feel a warm inner glow that seemed to be 'broadcasting' in the direction of my mind, as if my child were trying to tell me these were good things."

*A third change pregnancy brings is a propensity to turn inward—*another characteristic parapsychologists have associated with heightened intuition.

If she is like most women, the expectant mother becomes more introspective, contemplative. She may appear less rational and more moody, sometimes dreamy. Characteristically, thoughts and feelings may preoccupy her. She appears to be almost brooding. This distinctly pregnant turn of mind, often resulting in inattention to the world around her, has won her the stereotype of "flightiness." Along with her inner focus, however, her inner life becomes richer and more complex.

In itself, turning inward is not enough to create intuition from whole cloth. However, the expectant mother may notice the subtle and undramatic intuitive events that probably occur to all of us without our realizing it.

For instance, Gayle, a first-time mother and senior engineer in an architectural firm, describes a phenomenon familiar to many during the prenatal months. "It's as if someone switched a fine-tuning knob on my mind," she explains. "I felt more attuned to subtle feelings. I find myself suddenly thinking of my husband just before he calls even though he rarely phones at the same time each day."

Another expectant mother summed up the feelings of many: "I feel more tuned in," she says. Many mothers use such expressions as "fine-tuning" or "tuning in" to describe the state of mind conducive to intuition. But tuned in to what? The body? The inner mind? Perhaps something else science has only just begun to explore?

The fourth condition that may heighten the mother's intuition is her greater awareness of her body's rhythms and even subtle sensations. The mother experiences a heightened awareness of her unborn child just as she experiences heightened digestive sensitivity. This probably explains a great many pregnancy intuitions. But it hardly explains intuiting who is on the telephone before it rings. Or the gender of the unborn child.

Experts in the field of intuition development recommend quieting the mind and centering within. This is usually accomplished with relaxation exercises, guided imagery, and other methods, which we will explore in a later chapter. Expectant mothers, on the other hand, are already inner focused and may, therefore, already be attuned to this more subtle way of knowing.

A fifth change pregnancy brings that may account for heightened intuition is the expectant mother's greater right-brain hemisphere orientation. Dr. Ehrenwald says, "Psi is a right-hemisphere activity.[13] Put in a nutshell," Dr. Ehrenwald writes, "it could be stated that the right hemisphere presides over the three *I's*: intuition, inspiration, and imagination. It is the fount and origin of human creativity."[14]

According to psychologist Patricia Maybruck, Ph.D., who has done extensive research on the psychology of pregnancy, "Pregnancy is one of those times when the right brain becomes enhanced in women. It also seems fitting for the expectant mother to be especially preoccupied with such right-brain thoughts as creativity and nurturing."[15] She becomes more creative, in closer touch with her instincts, and closer to her emotions.

The left hemisphere is associated with reasoning, logic, and rational thinking. The right hemisphere, on the other side of the brain, connotes creative thinking, instinct, nonrational thought. The right hemisphere is also characterized by images and pictures, a factor that may account for the pregnant mother's frequent "dreaminess." Dominant right-hemisphere activity is associated with grasping an issue or concept in its entirety, namely, intuition. Most all professionals—from business executives to artists—benefit from combining right- and left-hemisphere ways of thinking. Experts in the field of parapsychology also believe that the right hemisphere is the center of extrasensory perception.

A sixth possible reason the expectant mother is more intuitive may lie in her heightened emotional sensitivity—a pregnancy change that causes no end of frustration to the mother's mate and close relatives. As just about every expectant father is all-too-aware, pregnancy triggers roller-coaster emotions. One minute the expectant mother is content with the world. She has a feeling of well-being. Everything is right. Then, for no clear reason, her emotions may abruptly make an about-face. A casual remark triggers a flood of feelings and brings her to tears. This familiar state is called *emotional lability* and often occurs even before pregnancy begins to show.

Nancy, a first trimester expectant mother says, "Things make me cry very easily, even the most trivial things—a particular phrase, an image, a thought, a tone of voice—things that don't normally make me upset."

These all-too-familiar mood swings are usually blamed on hormonal activity. However, a number of factors in addition to changing hormones contribute to pregnancy's emotional lability. At the root of the mother's increased sensitivity is probably a blend of psychological and physiological factors: her changing body image, her ambivalence about becoming a mother, fears about birth, concerns about the baby, thoughts of her changing relationship with her partner, physical discomforts, and of course the joy of feeling new life within. The mother-to-be's heightened sensitivity may help to attune her to the subtle voice of intuition that others rarely hear. In other words, her increased sensitivity may encompass more than emotional and psychological events. In fact, gifted psychics are sometimes called "sensitives" presumably because they are more sensitive to the world of ESP. Greater emotional receptivity may also make the mother more "parapsychologically sensitive."

As her center of energy shifts from left to right hemisphere, as she turns inward, paying more attention to thoughts and feelings than to the external world, the expectant mother may experience still another change that predisposes her to heightened intuition. It appears that the veil between conscious and unconscious becomes thinner, more permeable.

A seventh condition that probably accounts for the expectant mother's heightened intuition is her closeness to unconscious mental processes. In fact, this unique state of mind creates an opportunity for growth and development. The expectant mother may experience insights, spurts of self-growth. Pregnant women, psychologists have found, may be more open to change and long-term psychological healing during pregnancy than at other times.[16]

Eighth, as pregnancy rolls on, the expectant mother may also become closer to what psychologists call the collective unconscious—the world of myth, symbol, and archetype. This is the part of ourselves that transcends the personal ego. That part of our being, parapsychologists theorize, is the seat of intuition.

BEYOND THE PERSONAL

It is little wonder that thousands of years ago, nameless ancient artisans fashioned goddess figures in the shape of expectant mothers with expanded abdomens and pendulous breasts. These symbolic figures no doubt represent the power of creation, fertility, the source of life.

According to world-renowned psychologist Erich Neumann, Ph.D., "Figures of the Great Mother are representations of the pregnant goddess of fertility, who was looked upon throughout the world as the goddess of pregnancy and childbearing."[17] The large number of animal figures belonging to these representations shows that this figure of the Great Goddess of birth is the mother of all living things, of animals as well as men."[18]

Psychologists have noticed that today, millennia later, many expectant mothers find themselves identifying with such goddess figures and other archetypes of creation. For example, Leni Schwartz, Ph.D, a transpersonal psychologist (a psychologist who explores the relationship between the self and universal consciousness, i.e., beyond the personal ego) observes: "The transition into motherhood puts a woman in touch with the power of bearing life and in turn with the mythic mother principle that gives life to forms—the creative, the nurturing, the collaborative. She identifies with mythological figures: earth goddesses and the Universal, or Divine, Mother."[19] The connection with mythic images representing creation may occur at any time during pregnancy or labor.

Julie, a first-time mother in Arlington, Texas, recalls her experience of identifying with timeless images of creation. "During pregnancy the idea of goddess archetypes like the Willendorf Venus image took on a whole new dimension," Julie recalls.

"In our society where the emphasis is on a woman's sexual beauty and the 'perfect' thin and unmarred body, I've seen many of my friends get really depressed during and after pregnancy by the changes in their bodies. My identification with the sacred image of birth helped me avoid these feelings. When I got really huge, I had days where I felt like a whale. But most of the time I felt proud and fulfilled to be a part of the miracle of creating a new life. Remembering the goddess image made me feel special and empowered, instead of fat and ruined."

Another new mother, Margaret, who lives in Virginia, found herself thinking of similar images as her pregnancy progressed.

"I thought about the ancient goddess figures frequently during the final months of my last pregnancy as I grew bigger and bigger," she recalls. "It was comforting to me to think that voluptuous pregnant bodies were once revered. And it reminded me that I was going through a process as old as mankind and to enjoy being pregnant and take pride in my shape."

As pregnancy draws close to its climax in birth, the expectant mother frequently seems to be in touch with what psychologist Carl Jung has called the *collective unconscious*—a part of the self that may be linked with all life. As the barriers between self and the world beyond the personal ego seem to let down, many expectant mothers experience periods of *transpersonal awareness*—that is, an identification with something greater than ordinary life.

Many women feel as if they were mother of all life. Emily, a prominent New York editor, puts it this way: "I remember looking at homeless people on the street and getting very teary eyed to think of them as clean, fresh, tiny newborns."

During the procreative months or during labor, some expectant mothers experience a sense of oneness with nature, with all women who have ever given birth, or with all life. Dr. Schwartz describes this heightened awareness in her book *Bonding Before Birth*: "We are becoming increasingly aware that pregnancy and birth can precipitate transcendent, ecstatic emotional states, similar to those caused by other intense experiences such as orgasm or the creation of art, contact with nature, or a spiritual experience. She may transcend the ordinary, familiar sense of self to achieve an extraordinary understanding of being one with the cosmos."[20]

CHAPTER 4

COUVADE SYNDROME

While Dorothy was at home in West Virginia, her husband, Paul, was overseas during World War II. He wrote a most unusual letter. In the letter he said she was pregnant and he could feel it. Dorothy thought her husband was experiencing a peculiar mental aberration. She visited her doctor, however, just to be sure. To her amazement, she found Paul was right. She was pregnant and later gave birth to a baby boy.

Paul is not alone. His experience is common to many men. On some level, a few fathers experience pregnancy or childbirth. This experience suggests that, surprisingly, the metamorphosis of pregnancy may not be limited to mother and child. Expectant fathers may also experience the symptoms and signs of labor in a way no psychologist or physician understands.

THE RITE OF MALE CHILDBIRTH

The father's experience of pregnancy began in ancient times—perhaps as early as parents have been having babies. In many cultures—thousands of miles from one another and as distinct from each other as Borneo and China—expectant fathers have observed a unique and unusual childbirth custom.

Marco Polo witnessed the custom in China with the mountain tribe of the Miau-tse. The Greek writer Herodotus discussed it in his writings about African tribes. And the Roman writer Strabo related the phenomenon as it occurred among the Iberians in Spain.

Called *couvade* (from a French verb *couver* meaning "to hatch or brood"), the custom—as varied as the people who practice it—takes two basic forms. In one form of couvade, the father observes prenatal dietary restrictions, wears special clothing, or avoids polluting substances. For instance, in the Philippines, he stops eating sour fruit to prevent the child's getting a stomachache. In Borneo, he refrains from eating cork to prevent the child's constipation. In China, the father guards against violent movements to protect the growing embryo.[1] The other form of couvade is even more dramatic. The expectant father goes to bed and, depending on the culture, either mimics labor or actually seems to experience labor contractions.

Anthropologists and psychologists have suggested a variety of explanations for these customs. For example, some researchers have interpreted the couvade ritual as a gesture by the father to share fully in the act of creation.[2] Others have considered the rite a symbolic expression of the bond between father and child.[3] Some believe ritual couvade behavior stems from the father's envy of the mother's creative powers. Psychologist Bruno Bettelheim attributed ritual couvade to selfish behavior from the birth-envious father. In some cultures, the father takes to bed and compels the new mother to return immediately to work while he rests. Still others have suggested couvade rituals are rites of sympathetic magic during which the father deters evil spirits from his mate.[4] In any case, the ritual behavior represents the father's participation in the passage rite of birth. It's likely that this rite has different meanings for different cultures. Since there are so many forms of couvade behavior, all these interpretations may be correct. Or none of them.

THE FATHER'S EXPERIENCE OF PRENATAL SYMPTOMS

Can an expectant father really experience the physical symptoms of childbirth? There is little question that he often does just that. A surprising number of expectant fathers experience morning nausea, vomiting, abdominal pain, inexplicable weight gain, fatigue, dizziness, unusual food cravings, and other symptoms associated with pregnant women.

Dubbed *couvade syndrome* by British professor of psychiatry, W. H. Trethowan and consultant psychiatrist M. F. Conlon of the University of Birmingham, the father's experience of pregnancy symptoms remains one of the strangest, well-documented phenomenon in all medical literature.

COMMON PREGNANCY SYMPTOMS IN MEN

The following are the most common symptoms expectant fathers
may experience:

- Nausea
- other gastrointestinal complaints
- Unintentional weight gain
- Headaches
- Inexplicable fatigue

- Insomnia
- More frequent colds
- Inability to concentrate
- Restlessness
- Nervousness

Couvade syndrome is quite different from ritual couvade. It is not
mimicry. Rather, it's a male reaction to pregnancy—as involuntary as
the mother's morning sickness.

"Despite the chronological relationship of pregnancy to the occurrence of symptoms," Drs. Trethowan and Conlon write, "The link
between these events may not be perceived by the sufferer . . .[5] *Subjects were seldom aware that their symptoms bore a relationship to
approaching parenthood.*"[6]

Even stranger, the father may experience a prenatal discomfort in
place of his partner. Writing about prenatal nausea, the authors of a
well-known maternity nursing text, *Maternity Care: The Nurse and the
Family*, say that if the mother does not have symptoms, the expectant
father may.[7] Again, the father may not have any idea that his symptoms
have anything to do with pregnancy.

Many health professionals have since studied the mysterious couvade syndrome in detail. For example, Professor Jacqueline Clinton,
Ph.D., at the School of Nursing, University of Wisconsin in Milwaukee,
underwent the first systematic attempt to monitor both physical and
psychological symptoms of expectant fathers over the entire course of
pregnancy.[8]

After collecting information from fathers-to-be at lunar month inter-
vals, Dr. Clinton recorded no less than thirty-nine different pregnancy
symptoms. She found that "compared to nonexpectant men, expectant
fathers were found to experience significantly more frequent and serious episodes of colds, unintentional weight gain, numerous gastrointestinal discomforts, irritability, nervousness, inability to concentrate,

headache, restlessness, excessive fatigue, and insomnia during various trimesters of pregnancy and the early postpartum period."[9]

Other systematic studies have shown similar results. For example, Mack Lipkin, M.D., and his associate Gerri Lamb, M.S., of the Departments of Medicine and Psychiatry of the University of Rochester in New York, performed a unique study of expectant fathers' symptoms. They took an *epidemiologic* view—that is, an approach focusing on the history of an epidemic disease.

They researched what happened when expectant fathers sought medical care for couvade-type symptoms. The symptoms the men experienced were *all obvious pregnancy symptoms* one would think would be limited to expectant mothers. "One patient," report the researchers, "had chest pain that felt like 'something was pushing out.' He also had urinary burning and abdominal pain. His abdominal pain was described as 'sinking into the bladder.'" Few people, other than an expectant mother or obstetrician, could better describe the physical sensations of pregnancy.

What did health care providers do for these men? Since couvade symptoms are so common in expectant fathers, one would expect the health care provider to reassure the expectant dad that pregnancy may be the cause of his symptoms and that they would most likely vanish after birth. On the contrary, the health care providers prescribed a wide range of medical interventions. These included upper-gastrointestinal series, X rays, a gallbladder series, numerous blood tests, and the prescription of a veritable pharmacopoeia, ranging from codeine to Mylanta.

There is nothing wrong with medical tests in the face of suspected diseases. However, that the men with the symptoms were expectant fathers was noted on the medical records of only 15 percent (26) of the 179 men who sought health care. Considering that couvade syndrome is as widespread as it is, this seems nothing short of incredible. Even more remarkable, however, is that, as the researchers observed, "*In no case did the providers record recognition of a possible connection between the symptoms and the pregnancy.*"[10]

Given that couvade syndrome affects hundreds of thousands of men throughout the world yearly, it seems only reasonable for health professionals to ask expectant fathers and expectant mothers about their health problems during the childbearing season.[11] This would assess the father's health needs while simultaneously reassuring him that it is not

DETERMINING ILLNESS IN EXPECTANT FATHERS
DURING PREGNANCY

- Determine whether the symptom is a typical pregnancy symptom
- Consult a health care provider
- Report the symptom along with the fact that pregnancy is occurring in the family
- Be sure the health care provider rules out any other possible cause of the symptom
- Recognize that you are not "just imagining things"— inexplicable as it may be, pregnancy symptoms in men are very common
- Rest assured that in most cases, the pregnancy symptoms disappear shortly after birth

unusual for him to be experiencing inexplicable pregnancy symptoms. It would also provide a valuable opportunity to give the expectant father emotional support and counseling when needed as he undergoes the lifelong changes childbirth brings.[12] At the very least, health care providers should ask the men who report pregnancy-like symptoms if a pregnancy is occurring in the family.

What causes fathers to experience prenatal symptoms? How can a man's body experience changes that are obviously associated with his partner's pregnancy? Most medical professionals interpret couvade syndrome as a psychosomatic symptom, like experiencing "butterflies" in the belly before going to the dentist. Health professionals have suggested that symptoms result from emotional factors such as anxiety and envy of the mother's reproductive ability.

On the surface, this seems like a perfectly reasonable explanation. The father's irritability, insomnia, weight gain, nervousness, and a variety of other symptoms may very well stem from perfectly normal concerns and worries about becoming a father. Increasingly, we hear couples using the expression, "We are pregnant." This implies that both parents share the state of expectant parenthood. Like the mother, the father, too, is changing. He is preparing to adopt a new role in life; it is only natural to expect that he will also have emotional ups and downs. But does this explain symptoms of pregnancy? Is anxiety really the cause? In some cases it probably is. However, what about morning sickness? What about leg cramps? These are not traditional anxiety symptoms. And what about cases when the father experiences the symptoms *before* he realizes his mate is pregnant? Richard, an accountant working in a New York City firm, was suddenly stricken with nausea in the morning. He assumed he was coming down with the flu. His nausea continued for several days until it grew so intense he had to call in sick for work. When he discussed it with Susa, his wife, she said she had no flu symptoms. But her mate's nausea reminded her it might be a good idea to have a pregnancy test.

When the results came back, Susa was indeed pregnant.

PREGNANCY SYMPTOMS IN OTHERS

What about pregnancy symptoms in family members who are miles from the expectant mother? These can hardly be explained away as psychosomatic reactions.

Next to the mother, the father-to-be is the person most likely to experience pregnancy and labor symptoms. However, other members of the family and sometimes even health professionals occasionally undergo symptoms of the mother's pregnancy and labor.[13] Twins frequently report this peculiar phenomenon. There are dozens of cases in parapsychological literature when twins experience the same pains at the same time even when they are across the world from one another. For example, Maryanne, a mother, reports, "My mother who is a twin felt labor pains when her sister had her last child thousands of miles away. My mother did not know at the time that her sister was in labor."

When Alberta was giving birth in Minneapolis, Minnesota, her twin sister, Cora, who was vacationing in the Virgin Islands, was apparently feeling the contractions.

"I didn't speak to my twin sister, Cora, until a couple of days after the birth of my daughter," recalls Alberta. "When I finally spoke to her and announced the news, she told me that on the very night I was in labor, she was suddenly gripped by painful abdominal cramps. She first thought it was horrible menstrual cramps. Yet she was not having her period. When she found out I had been in labor, she knew this was the cause of her pain.

"Oddly, this was the first time we've had a psychic experience in many years. Cora and I have very little in common other than the fact that we are twin sisters."

Dr. Ian Stevenson, professor of psychiatry at the University of Virginia, reports another fascinating episode between two women, Dora and Martha, that occurred when Martha was pregnant.

While in Naples, Italy, Dora woke up with a pain in her chest and a terrible feeling of depression, "as if someone had put a cloak on my shoulders." Her husband, who is a physician, examined her and found nothing wrong physically. Three or four hours later, Dora's feeling passed. Then that evening she experienced pain she describes as feeling as though she had a collapsed lung. It was her physician husband who finally realized that Dora may have been experiencing her sister's pain. Later, Dora received a letter explaining that her sister Martha had given birth and experienced complications. The baby was in a transverse position, which caused *placenta previa* (a grave complication in which the placenta detaches from the uterine wall before the baby is born, and can result in severe blood loss). During the birth of her child, Martha developed blood clots throughout her body, localizing in her lungs.[14]

Clearly, these pregnancy symptoms are not merely the result of anxiety or some other psychosomatic factor. What then does cause prenatal symptoms in the father and others close to the mother?

THE MOST MYSTERIOUS FORM OF ESP

Is couvade a mysterious form of ESP?

Pregnancy symptoms in other family members including expectant fathers could be what parapsychologists call a *telesomatic symptom*— that is, a psi-mediated physiological response or "ESP of the body." By some process no one understands, ESP is translated into physical symptoms.

Parapsychologists have observed that crisis sometimes brings about extrasensory experiences. Could couvade syndrome be a form of "crisis ESP?" Could couvade syndrome sometimes be yet another paranormal dimension of pregnancy? Parapsychological investigator Rosalind Heywood reports a dramatic case of what may be a psi-mediated physiological response perhaps elicited by crisis. Five weeks before her due date, a woman in Israel gave birth, while thousands of miles away in

London, England, her own mother had a most inexplicable experience. She experienced what she describes as severe stomach cramps, lasting more than three hours. There was no reason for her to expect that her daughter had gone into premature labor.[15]

Psychiatrist Berthold Schwarz, M.D., has collected dozens of tele-somatic symptoms in his research of hundreds of cases of parent-child telepathy. In one remarkable episode, Dr. Schwarz reports of a young army wife unexpectedly hospitalized for threatened miscarriage. Her fifty-six-year-old mother, who had two daughters and was hundreds of miles away, developed uterine bleeding at the same time. This was not an isolated incident for her. She experienced similar inexplicable bleed-ing when her other daughter went into labor, even though labor occurred seven weeks before her expected date of birth. As is often the case with expectant fathers who experience pregnancy or labor symp-toms, the mother was unaware of the relationship between her own symptoms and her daughter's obstetric experiences. Yet, as Dr. Schwarz points out, these episodes of uterine bleeding "coincided with major obstetrical changes in the lives of her two daughters."[16]

Telesomatic symptoms are by no means limited to pregnancy. A famous religious example of a probable telesomatic symptom is the appearance of the *stigmata* (physical marks resembling the wounds of the crucifixion), occurring in certain individuals throughout Catholic his-tory. Though the stigmata is quite rare, physical symptoms apparently caused paranormally—that is, because of telepathy or some other phe-nomenon we do not understand—are more common than most people realize. Louisa Rhine, a famous parapsychological researcher, reported ten thousand cases of spontaneous psychic experiences. Of these 169 cases (1.7 percent) were paranormally perceived physical symptoms.[17]

Psychiatrist Carl Jung experienced an astounding telesomatic expe-rience of his own.

He writes: "At about two o'clock, I woke up with terror and was convinced that someone had come into the room. . . . Then I tried to think back, and it seemed that I had been awakened with a dull pain, as if something had struck against my forehead and had pushed against the back of my skull." The next day, Dr. Jung received a telegram bear-ing tragic news. One of his patients had shot himself. The bullet had lodged at the back of the skull."[18]

Marti, a software engineer, describes feeling her mother's symptoms when she was a little girl: "One night at a Girl Scout meeting my thumb started to throb for no apparent reason. Several people at the meeting saw me holding my thumb and asked about it. When a neighbor picked me up (my mother usually did this) she told me my mother was at the hospital getting stitches after cutting her thumb."

Medical literature refers to numerous instances of one person experiencing the pain of another. This is most common among family members or those with a close emotional tie. For example, Louisa Rhine records an example of a woman stricken with intense chest pains who later received a telegram that her closest girlfriend had died of a heart attack at the time her experience occurred.[19]

Several clinical studies have clearly shown a telesomatic response in a controlled laboratory setting. For example, physicist Douglas Dean, Ph.D., undertook some of the most fascinating research in history regarding medical paranormal phenomena. In well-controlled laboratory tests, he showed that subjects hooked to a *plethysmograph* (a device used to measure blood volume changes in body extremities) registered physical changes in heart rate and blood flow in response to telepathic signals. His experiments were done with pairs of individuals. One person acted as a "sender," who focused on a thought or image; the other was the "receiver" who was hooked up to the plethysmograph in another room. Dr. Dean used cards with fifteen names, five from the telephone directory, five chosen by the subject, and five chosen by the agent, or sender. When the agent focused his or her attention on names chosen by the subject, the subjects' plethysmograph readings registered a significant dip, showing vasoconstriction. In one dramatic case, when a sender looked at a card symbolizing "mother," the receiver (in a different room) experienced transient *tachycardia* (increased heart rate) and change in vasoconstrictive state.[20]

Physiological ESP often occurs even when the recipient of the intuitive experience is not aware of the fact. For example, Dr. Charles Tart, professor of psychology at the University of California at Davis, conducted an unusual experiment with mild electric shocks. He administered shocks to a subject in a soundproof chamber. When receiving the shock, the subject attempted to send a message telepathically to a person (recipient) in another soundproof chamber several rooms away. The recipient was often unaware of the telepathic message received. However, electronic equipment detected brain wave and heart rate changes![21]

Perhaps by joining hands with parapsychology, obstetrics may one day understand more about the father's experience of pregnancy. One can easily understand why pregnancy can influence the father, sometimes in a dramatic way. He, too, has an unseen connection with his unborn child. Becoming a parent is a life-changing experience for fathers as well as mothers.

Yet, like many mysteries of childbearing, the couvade syndrome is a phenomenon that medical science does not and probably never will fully understand.

CHAPTER 5

THOUGHTS: MUSIC OF THE UNBORN

The most mysterious facets of pregnancy occur in utero.

A universe is born within a mother's womb sometime between the fourteenth and eighteenth week of pregnancy. A pregnancy milestone, the event is often called "quickening" because it suddenly seems as if life were breathed into the mysterious depths of the womb. After feeling those first butterfly sensations of her baby, the mother's thoughts turn inward. She thinks, dreams, fantasizes, and even communicates on a nonverbal level with her unborn child.

The expectant father, too, may share a rapport with his preborn child. As with most pregnancy experiences, however, he usually lags weeks behind his mate. After all, he does not feel the turnings and kicks or have the constant reminder of the baby's presence. Typically, the expectant father's thoughts turn to the baby when the visible signs of pregnancy appear. For many men the turning point occurs when, hand on his mate's abdomen, he can first feel the baby move. That is when pregnancy stops being just a big belly and becomes "our child."

Long before either parent senses her motion, the preborn child migrates about the womb. She takes her first journey immediately after conception. After uniting in microscopic matrimony in one of the fallopian tubes, sperm and egg form a tiny new being (called the *ovum* for the first two weeks after conception) who begins a three-day journey to the womb.

The ovum travels through the fallopian tube. Also called *oviduct*, each fallopian tube extends from the ovaries four to five inches to either side of the uterus. Minute hairlike structures (*tubal cilia*) and waves of involuntary contractions called *peristalsis* assist the developing baby on its way to the womb. During its journey, the ovum undergoes a remarkable metamorphosis more amazing than caterpillar to butterfly. The cells divide. Within three days of conception it becomes a mulberrylike structure called *morula*—Latin for "mulberry" or "blackberry."

The little "blackberry" becomes a fluid-filled sphere with cells arranged toward the wall of the sphere. This structure is called by the rather unattractive name *blastocyst*. Toward one end of the blastocyst is grouped a mass of cells, called the *inner cell mass*. Though this inner cell mass is only a small portion of the dot which is the ovum, it will become your child. As the ovum changes, mother prepares to nurture her child. Her uterine lining becomes thick and succulent, ready to receive the developing ovum. After conception, this lining is called *decidua*—Latin for "falling down"—because, like the leaves of deciduous trees, the lining falls away and is shed after the baby is born.

Once in the womb, the new being floats freely for about four days. By the seventh day it is smaller than a carrot seed—tiniest of garden seeds—so small it is barely visible to the naked eye. This is when she implants on the uterine wall like a seed planted in fertile soil. Tiny rootlike projections called *chorionic villi* grow from the outer cells of what now appears as a shaggy cellular ball and begin burrowing into the uterine lining. Down, down the roots burrow like the roots of a tree growing into the soil until they tap the maternal bloodstream—source of life, oxygen, nourishment.

The amazing transformation continues.

The ovum becomes baby—membranes and amniotic fluid surrounding it—umbilical cord, and even placenta. Over the next nine months the new baby grows to 200 billion times its original mass. For the first eight weeks of life, the baby is called an *embryo*. During the embryonic period, the foundation for all organs and organ systems is laid.

As the embryo grows, mother and child are so closely united, so intimately fused, it is hard to distinguish mother from offspring. For instance, the disk-shaped placenta (from a Latin word meaning "cake") is a joint creation; part develops from the ovum and part from the decidua on the uterine wall.

Nine months before Mom and Dad capture their child's image in the family album, a strange alchemy takes place. It is as if the evolution of life on earth were being played on fast forward on the inner stage of the womb. The baby changes. From shaggy cellular ball to a fishlike being complete with gills, to something that looks like a curved salamander with a tail. And changes. By the time it is the size of a lima bean (the sixth week after conception), its face begins to appear. And its toes and fingers are webbed like duck's feet. As it changes again and again, she floats freely in a clear celestial bubble called the amniotic sac. Its own private universe.

The seventh week marks a turning point. The being—no larger than a date—looks almost like a tiny child. All organ systems are made. The embryonic period is complete. Now that it resembles a person from the eighth week until birth, the baby is called *fetus*, from a Latin word meaning "offspring." It has its own fingerprints, it is able to swallow, squint, frown, open and shut its mouth, move its arms and legs, even kick. And all of this takes place before the mother even begins to feel that gentle fluttering like the wings of a baby bird cupped in the palm of a hand.

A NEW VIEW OF THE UNBORN

Odd as it may appear, until just recently branches of medicine from psychology to pediatrics harbored a series of false and rather fantastic assumptions about this growing being.

STRIKING FACTS ABOUT THE UNBORN

Recent research may reveal that what pediatricians, obstetricians, and psychologists of a decade ago knew about unborns may be an incomplete story, if not outright fiction.

New discoveries reveal that unborns can do the following:

- Recognize Mom's and Dad's voice
- Recognize objects in utero
- Hear and respond to music
- Hear, respond to, and remember stories
- Communicate preverbally with both parents

For example, psychologists believed that newborns were virtually mindless and void of memory. Many scientists, from Sigmund Freud to Jean Piaget, estimated that the baby had no sense of objects until around eighteen months (despite its prenatal memories of playing with the umbilical cord and remembering a snakelike thing in the womb suggest that object recognition may commence in utero).[1] Neurologists erroneously believed that birth memory was impossible (despite that people have experienced birth memory and have been writing about it for decades!). Pediatricians mistakenly believed that newborns were all but blind (though any observer can see the intense gaze when infant and mother lock eyes for the first time!). And obstetricians believed (incredibly) that babies in utero felt no pain.

How can medicine be characterized by such a virtual fantasy world about infants?

One reason may be that most medical studies are done in the artificial environment of the hospital, which no doubt profoundly influences infant and maternal behavior. For example, studies of infants frequently follow an infant born in a drug-induced haze resulting from medications given the mother during labor. The infant is therefore not as alert as a child born after a natural birth. Other rituals of obstetrics, many of which are perishing as more women opt for more humanized birth, include transport from room to room during labor; a battery of obstetrical procedures such as internal electronic monitoring requiring scalp electrode implantation in utero; rupture of protective amniotic membranes; injections; giving birth in the supine position, in which the mother must push against gravity; maternal-infant separation; and artificial feeding.

Fortunately, our view of the unborn child is rapidly changing. Dr. William Liley, professor in the Postgraduate School of Obstetrics and Gynecology at the University of Auckland, New Zealand, observes: "Recent advances in fetal diagnosis and therapy have provided both the technology and opportunity to piece together a new picture of the fetus."[2] In fact, research reveals that the baby may be conscious and capable of learning, communicating, and even of amazing paranormal feats when not much bigger than a tadpole!

The unborn child may even experience cognitive thought. According to radiologist Jason Birnholz, M.D., who did an ultrasound imaging study at Harvard Medical School, REM sleep occurs in preborn babies as early as twenty-three weeks.[3] REM sleep is associated with dreaming, which is a cognitive activity.

LULLABY OF THE WOMB

The unborn child hears and responds to music and stories. Though many people think of the uterus as a silent and dark chamber, audio recordings of intrauterine sounds show that the primal security of baby's private macrocosm is anything but quiet. Before birth, the unborn child hears the rhythmic lulling sounds of mother's heartbeat, the rushing sound of moving fluid, and pulsations in the umbilical cord.

This lullaby of the womb continues to soothe after the baby is born. A group of Japanese physicians, Drs. Murooka, Koie, and Suda, completed a research project that should interest every parent of a crying baby. They recorded intrauterine sounds, then played the recording to newborns. Intrauterine sounds, they discovered, had a calming effect on newborns, lulling them to sleep.[4] A full 85 out of every 100 infants who listened to the intrauterine sounds stopped crying within thirty seconds of hearing the recording!

YOUR UNBORN CHILD'S FAVORITE SOUNDS

Pleasant sounds similar to those heard in utero can be used to calm a crying baby days, weeks, and sometimes even months after birth.
Here are some of your preborn baby's favorites:

- Mother's heartbeat
- Other intrauterine sounds (such as the swishing sound of fluids through the umbilical cord)
- Mother's and father's voice
- Soft relaxing music

Well known psychologist Lee Salk points out: "All the drum rhythms in the world belong to one or other of two basic patterns—either the rapid tattoo of animal hooves or the measured beat of the human heart ... the heart beat rhythm is more widespread in the world—even in groups like the Plains Indians who hunted the great herds of bison. Is this rhythm deeply imprinted on human consciousness from fetal life?"[5]

Apparently so. Dr. Salk launched a revealing research project focusing on the mother's heartbeat. The idea came when he noticed the majority of mothers he observed holding their babies on the left side whether they were left or right-handed. When he asked women why they chose this position, the left-handed mothers were inclined to say, "I'm left-handed and can hold my baby better this way," whereas the right-handed mothers answered, "I'm right-handed and when I hold my baby on the left side it frees my right hand to do other things."

It is unlikely that right- and left-handed mothers were doing the same thing for different reasons. The mothers, thought Dr. Salk, may have been giving a rationalization for an automatic response that was not related to hand preference. He made a study of paintings and sculpture that portrayed a mother holding a child. He found that throughout the world in all periods of history, four out of five of these artworks showed the mother holding the baby on her left side.

Meanwhile, psychiatrist Hyman Weiland, M.D., of the Northridge Psychiatric Medical Group, Northridge, California, noticed the same phenomenon among mothers at a well-baby clinic. Mothers markedly preferred the left side. As a control, he observed shoppers carrying packages approximately the size of a baby. Half held the package on the left and half held it on the right.[6] So there is something special about holding a baby. When a mother holds her infant on her left side, she places the baby close to her heart, closest to the sound the infant has heard before birth.

Dr. Salk divided first-time mothers into two groups and found that those who were separated from their infant after birth had a tendency to hold their baby on the right side whereas those who remained with the child immediately after birth held their baby on the left. Apparently, the "holding response" was established during the first twenty-four hours after birth, an especially sensitive time for the development of maternal-infant attachment. Unconsciously and automatically, the mother seems to sense that her baby will be calmed when held close to her heart.

To confirm the soothing power of maternal heart tones, Dr. Salk divided babies in a hospital nursery into three groups. He played maternal heart tones at the normal rate heard in utero (72 beats per minute) to one group; he played heart tones at an accelerated 128 beats per minute to another group. Yet another group acted as control, hearing no heart tone recordings. The majority who heard the normal maternal heart sounds gained more weight, slept better, and cried less than those who did not hear the sounds. Those who listened to the rapid heart tones became so upset that the recording had to be stopped.[7]

Intrauterine sounds are not the only sounds your unborn child hears. Throughout prenatal development, your unborn child hears the words you speak, the music you play, and even the clamor of traffic. Dr. Ethan Zimmer and a group of medical researchers from the Uni-

versity of Florida at Gainesville studied the passage of sound from outside to inside the pregnant uterus. They came up with clear evidence
that a variety of sounds comes through the uterus loud and clear and
that the unborn child definitely reacts to these sounds.[8] According to
an article in the British Medical Journal, *Lancet*, infants relaxed to soap
opera theme music they heard regularly during the prenatal period.
Researchers studied newborn response to the theme song of a soap
opera four to five days after birth. Infants whose mothers had watched
the soap opera during pregnancy adopted a quiet alert state when hearing the theme song.[9]

Babies show marked preferences for certain types of music.

For a Ph.D. dissertation, Dr. Roberta Panneton, a student of
Anthony DeCasper, professor of psychology at the University of North
Carolina, asked expectant mothers to sing "Mary Had a Little Lamb"
every day toward the end of pregnancy. After birth, the babies preferred
this melody to an unfamiliar one. They calmed down and showed more
interest in the melody. Meanwhile, a control group of newborns who
had not had been consistently exposed to a melody during pregnancy
showed no preference.[10]

Like adults, babies yet unborn have definite likes and dislikes in
music. One three year old who spontaneously remembered his life in
the womb said he didn't like the low notes in the folk songs his mother
sang during pregnancy.[11] "During my first pregnancy," Nisa, an Australian mother recalls, "I went to a concert that to my tastes I should
have enjoyed, but I felt physically ill, and the baby never stopped doing
somersaults for a moment."

As one might imagine, classical music has a more soothing effect
on the unborn baby than rock. Toronto psychiatrist Thomas Verny, pioneer in the field of prenatal psychology, points out that the fetal heart
rate is steadied to the background of Vivaldi and Mozart, whereas rock
music drove the baby to violent kicking. Expectant mothers have
reported leaving rock concerts because the baby began kicking so vio-
lently. For example, in Essex, England, during a very loud rock concert, a baby in utero kicked so hard that the mother went home with a
broken rib![12] Another expectant mother had to leave a theater because
her baby kicked so hard during a movie about the Vietnam war.[13]

The preborn child becomes accustomed to the sounds the mother
hears. For example, an unusual Japanese research project showed that
babies whose mothers lived near the Osaka airport for at least the last
five months of pregnancy showed little or no reaction to jet planes over-

head, whereas others who weren't accustomed to airplane noise cried and seemed upset.[14] Meanwhile, getting acclimated to the noise does not necessarily make a baby immune from the effects of it. Drs. Ando and Hattori found that average birth weight of babies in the airport area was clearly less than the weight of those from other neighboring quieter areas.[15]

Angi, a mother of three in Seattle, recalls: When I was pregnant with my third child, I was anemic and, with such a low energy level, often played *The Little Mermaid*, a Disney animated musical, to keep my children busy while I dozed on the couch. After Susan was born, every time she heard that tape, she relaxed, looked happy and slightly surprised, and even turned her head to locate the source. *The Little Mermaid* would calm her when upset, even when nursing and walking failed."

STORIES TOLD IN UTERO

Perhaps the most important sound your child hears are the voices of Mom and Dad. By birth, the newborn knows and prefers her mother's and often father's voice. Dr. Henry Truby, professor of pediatrics, linguistics, and anthropology at the University of Miami, Florida, was a pioneer in recording the first infant cries by *spectroscopy* (an elaborate voiceprint). At only twenty eight weeks gestational age, he found that the voiceprint of a baby's cry could already be matched with that of his or her mother. This was early evidence that babies were learning their "mother" tongue in the womb.[16]

Anthony DeCasper, professor of psychology at the University of North Carolina, and William Fifer, another psychologist, conducted a fascinating experiment showing that newborns preferred their mother's voice over other female voices. They recorded new mothers reading the Dr. Seuss story *To Think I Saw It on Mulberry Street*. The infants, in bassinets, were equipped with earphones and a special nipple. By changing their suckling speed on the nipple, the newborn could switch from the mother's taped voice to the voice of another woman reading the same story. Newborns consistently preferred their own mother's voice.[17]

A similar research project reveals that newborns and even young children show a preference for stories they have heard while still in utero. Dr. DeCasper and Melanie Spence directed a most unusual experiment involving another Dr. Seuss story. They asked mothers to read *The Cat in the Hat* twice a day during the last six weeks of pregnancy. Within a few days of birth, they played recordings of two stories: the story told in the womb and another Dr. Seuss story. Again, as in the newborn study, the babies were set up with a special nipple. They could change the story from one to the other by adjusting suckling speed. Ten out of twelve newborns adjusted suckling speed to switch to the story they had heard in the womb.[18]

Tales told in utero may linger in memory for years. One father read aloud J. R. R Tolkien's *Hobbit* to his wife when she was six months' pregnant. He had forgotten this until his son was four years old and he began reading him the same book. Suddenly his son said, "Daddy, I've heard this story before!" The father insisted that he had not read the story, until the boy interrupted several times. Then his wife reminded him that he had read it aloud . . . before his son was born![19]

THOUGHTS AND THE UNBORN CHILD

Throughout pregnancy, the unborn child shares its mother's world. It reacts to hot and cold, sweet and bitter tastes, and the mother's fears and joys. It is well nourished when its mother is, it smokes with her, has cocktails with her, experiences her sadness, her love, her stress, her anger, her excitement, and may even share her thoughts. During pregnancy mother and baby are one body. The inseparable pair are attuned both physically and psychically. The rapport is so subtle that it is difficult if not sometimes impossible to separate ESP from physiology. Perhaps mother and child share a synchronous relationship with both physiological and paranormal components.

More than a millennia ago, Chinese folk wisdom encouraged mothers to communicate healthy thoughts to the child in the womb, the idea being that positive thoughts and feelings influence the unborn child.[20] Modern obstetrics still has a long way to catch up with ancient Chinese folklore. Recent research reveals that positive thoughts and warm emotions may influence the unborn child as surely as good prenatal health habits.

A team of researchers studied what happens to the unborn child's breathing when the pregnant mother drinks alcohol. A group of expectant mothers each drank one ounce of 80-proof vodka in a glass of diet ginger-ale. The baby's breathing movements in utero were monitored by ultrasound scan and videotaped. Breathing movements decreased shortly after the mother drank the cocktail.[21] This is probably the result of the depressant effects of alcohol on the baby's central nervous system. For a similar reason, the baby's intrauterine breathing movements are decreased when the expectant mother takes narcotics such as Demorol.[22] Medical studies have shown that the unborn child's breathing movements are also inhibited when the mother smokes. Nicotine decreases the amount of oxygen available to the baby via the placenta.[23] All of these reactions result from a direct physical stimulus: the effects of drugs on the developing central nervous system.

Most mothers realize that dietary habits, including smoking and drinking, affect their unborn child. What many do not realize, however, is emotions and thoughts may also reach the preborn as surely as do food and fluids. An extraordinary study conducted by Dr. Michael Lieberman showed the mother did not have to light up a cigarette to affect her preborn child. Just *thinking* of smoking caused an increase in fetal heart rate.[24]

ESP? This phenomenon can probably be explained without recourse to the paranormal. Perhaps anticipating lighting a cigarette causes a rise in the mother's heart rate the unborn child can hear. Or stress hormones released at the thought of smoking may be transmitted via the placenta to the fetus and initiate an increased heart rate. The same subtle mechanisms may be involved in conveying the mother's anxiety before an amniocentesis—a diagnostic procedure in which a small quantity of fluid is drawn off from the uterus via a needle through the abdominal and uterine walls. While waiting for an ultrasound done with amniocentesis, babies become more active than they do when just waiting for a routine ultrasound.[25] The preborn child, it is likely, is reacting to the mother's stress.

Lester Sontag, M.D., of the Fels Research Institute, has researched the effect of emotional disturbance on the unborn child. In nine mothers who suffered traumatic incidents ranging from a mate's death to other emotional disturbances, fetal activity (suggesting the unborn child's agitation) "rose precipitously by a factor of approximately ten times its previous level."[26]

Pediatrician Barry Zuckerman, M.D., did a revealing study at Boston City Hospital to find the relationship between an expectant mother's depression and later irritability in the newborn. He and his colleagues examined more than eleven hundred mothers who were depressed during pregnancy. The researchers discovered that the babies of depressed mothers not only cried more and were more difficult to console, but the greater the mother's depression, "the more likely it was that the infant would be inconsolable or cry excessively." Moreover, their excessive crying was directly proportionate to their mother's depression scores![27] In concluding, the researchers point out that "emotions and neonatal behavior may be inextricably linked, even before delivery."[28]

David Cheek, M.D., a retired obstetrician formerly practicing in the San Francisco Bay area and Fellow of the American College of Surgeons, The American College of Obstetricians and Gynecologists, and the American Society of Clinical Hypnosis, has done extensive research on prenatal experiences. He has observed, "Women who are happily married and are pleasurably excited about the fact of their pregnancy generally give birth without difficulty to healthy children who adapt well to the vicissitudes of life."[29]

This does not mean that women who are not in an ideal life situation cannot also raise healthy, well-adjusted children. The point is that the mother's emotions influence her preborn child.

IMPOSSIBLE MEMORIES

In 1983, a team of researchers in Canada and the United States joined hands with innovative psychiatrist Thomas Verny, M.D., to study the world of the unborn. They organized the Association for Perinatal Psychology and Prenatal Health (APPAPH). This organization has made discoveries about the little known world of the preborn child that may very well change the way we think about preborns, babies, and birth. One of the most remarkable of these discoveries came to light during the hypnotherapy work of psychologist David Chamberlain, Ph.D.

One late summer afternoon in 1975, one of Dr. Chamberlain's clients, in hypnosis, suddenly announced, "I see my birth! The doctor is holding me up, laughing, saying, 'See, I told you it would be a girl.'"

Amazing, thought Dr. Chamberlain. How can a newborn baby who has never heard a spoken word remember the specific words said at its birth, to say nothing of the meaning behind the words? The birth experience must be a fantasy: a woman's mental creation of what she imagined her birth to be. Or was it? Dr. Chamberlain was determined to find out. Was birth memory fact or fantasy? Or a combination of both?

For the next five years, he labored through a research project whose results cannot be explained by anything medical science knows about babies, the body, the brain, or the mind. With his clients' permission, he began to tape and transcribe hundreds of birth reports. As he collected birth memories, he came up with an ingenious way to verify them for accuracy. He decided to hypnotize pairs of mothers and children, separately, and compare their reports of the child's birth. Mothers said they had never discussed these details with the children, and the children, most of them in their teens, had no conscious recollection of their birth. The results from ten pairs are nothing less than astounding.

Many of the birth memories he collected were baffling for the number of sheer details that seem impossible for a newborn—to say nothing of a preborn—to recall. Details included accurate descriptions of the birth process; whether or not forceps and other instruments had been used; the time of day; the layout of the birth room; who held or spoke to the baby first; the appearance of the plastic bassinet; feedings with water, formula, or breast milk; and even word-for-word conversations that took place at the birthsite.

Mothers' and children's reports generally dovetailed well. In a few cases where reports disagreed, the child turned out to be right. For example, in one pair, a boy talked about the color of the car his parents used to drive him home from the hospital. The mother reported a different color. When Dr. Chamberlain asked her about this later, she suddenly recalled that the child was right. She had reported the color of her own car. But it turned out that the newborn was driven home in his grandmother's car.

There is nothing new about remembering one's own birth. Birth memories have surfaced in several forms of therapy and altered states of consciousness, including psychoanalysis, hypnosis, hypnotherapy, primal therapy, LSD-induced altered mind states, and yoga. Psychoanalyst Otto Rank, an early associate of Freud, believed that most all psychological problems stemmed from one's birth experience.[30] He even went so far as to say that swinging was popular because it repeated the rhythm felt in the womb. His ideas are considered as radical today as they were in the early part of the century.

Parents occasionally come across a child's spontaneous memory of birth. In fact, Dr. Chamberlain points out, "skeptical parents sometimes come to accept birth memory when they hear their two year olds' spontaneously talking about it."[31] For example, during a long car trip, a three-year-old Wisconsin boy suddenly asked his mother if she remembered the day he was born. Then he went on to tell her it was dark inside and he was up high and could not get through the door. "I was scared, so I finally jumped and got through the door. Then I was okay."

This was an accurate description of the real event. During the mother's labor, the baby really was stuck high in the mother's pelvis for a long labor then finally "charged" through the "door" in a ten-minute second-stage labor (second stage is the birth process, with an average length of 30 to 120 minutes).[32]

Admittedly it is often difficult, if not impossible, to distinguish genuine memory from fantasy. What may appear to be a real memory may sometimes turn out to be a metaphor for feelings. However, some memories include details that can hardly be explained away as fantasy. When one man asked his daughter what it was like before she was born, she assumed the frank breech position (buttocks, rather than head, first) she had been in before birth. Another child talks about "a snake, but not a poisonous snake," in the womb with her.[33] The "snake" appears to be the umbilical cord.

THE PARANORMAL UNBORN

If memories of birth are impressive, memories of the life in the womb boggle the mind. Loretta, one of Dr. Chamberlain's clients, remembered, in hypnotherapy, an occurrence that took place while she was in the womb. In her third trimester of pregnancy, her mother was standing on a boat deck tightly holding the railing.

Loretta recalls: "She's looking at an island. There are other people looking over the water, listening to someone tell them where they are going, explaining to them about the island. My father is standing by my mother, worried about her. He wants to know if she is all right. The rocking of the boat is making her sick. She sat down and is rubbing her stomach. I feel the motion on the stomach, the rubbing. My mother was rubbing me, and she was worried if I was all right."

Loretta's parents said the event took place as Loretta reported it while they were on a sightseeing boat. They had never told her about the experience. And as Dr. Chamberlain adds, "Even if they had, it would not explain the empathy, perception, and clairvoyance found in her report."[34]

Dr. David Cheek has done extensive research on extrasensory perception in the womb. He has hypnotized many children and brought them back in memory to life before birth.

"Astonishing as it may be," he says, "there is no question that children are often able to remember details of the pregnancy. Such details include events, precise conversations, and even the description of places the parents have visited. This is utterly inexplicable in terms of conventional science. It implies that the unborn may be sometimes capable of understanding words he has never learned and has an ability that can only be called clairvoyance."

A newborn baby with pneumonia not only understood but later recalled the meaning of the words spoken shortly after birth in the hospital. "They're worried," she later recalled in therapy with Dr. David Chamberlain. "Got to watch it, make sure it doesn't get worse. They're going to leave somebody there. They could lose me. That's what they said."[35]

With hypnotized clients, Dr. Cheek uses an ideomotor technique based on bodily signals. This is because hypnotized people have difficulty verbalizing but are able to give muscular response with facial expressions to indicate pleasure, displeasure, surprise, and fear. He teaches his clients to use finger signals (which he compares to unconscious yes or no head movements).

YOUR UNBORN CHILD'S ESP

Adults and children under hypnosis have recalled mind-boggling ESP experiences that occurred while they were yet unborn.

The most common forms of ESP in unborn babies include the following:

- *Telepathy*—including understanding the spoken words of adults
- *Clairvoyance*—seeing objects and events outside the uterus
- *Out-of-body experiences*—seeing people, objects, and things as if from someplace outside the womb
- *Memories* (from conception to early abortion attempts) occurring before the brain or nervous system was formed

---

In one incredible case, Debbie, a thirteen-year-old girl under hypnosis with her mother, reports a clairvoyant experience she had in the second trimester of her mother's pregnancy with her. At first, Debbie recalled with uncertainty being inside the womb. "I guess I'm inside," she said. Then, encouraged by Dr. Cheek, she recalled details with such clarity that it almost transcends belief.

"Mother is sitting on the couch knitting something. My dad comes into the room and asks, 'Why are you knitting something for a *girl*?'"

Mimicking her mother's voice, Debbie said: "My Mother is saying, 'It's a girl. I know it's a girl. It *has* to be a girl!'"

At this point, Dr. Cheek asked Debbie a question no unborn child could possibly know let alone remember. He asked what her mother was wearing at the time of the event.

And Debbie answered.

"She has on a green plaid dress. I can't see any other color. I think it is dark."

With that extraordinary statement, Debbie's mother came out of hypnosis. She exclaimed. "I had a green-and-black plaid dress on and I can remember when that was! I had just begun feeling Debbie kicking. It was in April. I gave that dress away right after my pregnancy. I would have been almost five months along. That's incredible!"[36]

Conventional knowledge about pregnancy and the developing fetus does not even hint at explaining how such a memory is possible. We know that a preborn child can hear and perhaps even recognize her parents' voices. But how can a fetus at eighteen weeks' gestation whose brain is just developing recall and understand the meaning of the words his parents speak? For that matter, how can an unborn child know what color clothing her mother is wearing? To account for such memory, a baby not yet born must have clairvoyant powers so sophisticated that it is able to observe *from a place outside the womb*.

If this were one isolated case, it might be tempting to discount it as fiction, a deliberate hoax, or perhaps even an incredible coincidence. However psychologists and obstetricians have reported dozens of similar cases during which the preborn child accurately sees and recalls details that take place outside the uterus.

A thirty-four-year-old biologist under hypnosis with Dr. Cheek recalled details of his mother's pregnancy and labor with him. He remembered his grandmother sitting on a sofa with his mother crying after his grandfather died suddenly of a heart attack. And, as if observing from outside the womb, he described his mother's gray-and-white-striped maternity dress with a flower pattern, a round collar, and a pink bow around the neck. The mother later verified that she was wearing the dress her son described. The biologist also describes his mother's labor stopping. "My mother is afraid of dying, like her father. I'm stuck and they are trying to put forceps on my head." Dr. Cheek observes,

"He did not consciously know the fact that uterine contractions will stop when a mother is frightened."[37]

While eliciting birth memories from hypnotized clients, Dr. Cheek frequently observed clients repeating the head and shoulder movements that took place while negotiating through the birth passage! During a normal headfirst presentation in the birth outlet, as the head descends toward the outlet, it rotates so that the crown will enter the greatest diameter of the outlet. Then, as the head emerges, it will extend as though the baby were looking up. This results from the concave curve of the maternal sacrum. After coming through the vagina, the head rotates usually toward the mother's left side. This sequence of maneuvers is hardly something a person will mimic by accident!

AWESOME MEMORY SIGNS

Prenatal and birth memories have been verified in some of the following ways:

- Confirming the details with the parents or others present
- Repeating the actual positions assumed in utero or during the birth process
- Physical signs such as marks made by forceps and other instruments reappearing

---

Vaginally born children recalled the movements with accuracy. Cesarean-born children (who do not have such head and shoulder movements during the birth process) did not recall any postural changes. After reviewing the muscular sequences of close to 500 people, Dr. Cheek concludes: "There can be no question about the ability of babies to retain memory for the postural changes occurring during birth. No adult other than an obstetrician or obstetrical nurse would have been taught or talked about the mechanisms involved in a normal vaginal delivery."[38] In a similar vein, a Russian psychiatrist, Vladimir Raikov, showed that deeply regressed subjects displayed a wide range of neonatal reflexes. These were impossible to duplicate by hypnotic suggestion alone or by role-playing by professional actors.[39]

Bewildering physical signs sometimes suddenly appear along with prenatal memories. As Dr. Chamberlain observes: "An awesome sign of memory is the appearance of forceps bruises or a blue area on the throat where a person was being choked by the umbilical cord! That these marks come and go with the memory is a sure sign that memory has been preserved somewhere."[40] As uncommon and inexplicable as the phenomena are, several hypnotherapists and other researchers have observed these marks together with prenatal memories. This peculiar phenomenon of physical signs appearing during hypnotherapy may be some sort of little understood psychosomatic reaction. It has inspired some scientists to suggest that memory is in the very cells of the body.

Another woman recalls her pregnant mother talking with her brother about the soon-to-be-coming child. "He's asking, am I a boy or a girl? We'll find out when I'm born in about two weeks. She says if I am a girl my name will be Kimberly Sue. She doesn't know what it will be if I'm a boy."[41]

Perhaps the most incredible and heart-rending womb memories spotlight abortion attempts. Irene, one of Dr. Chamberlain's clients, remembered such an experience with striking, almost unbelievable detail.

"I was hardly formed and my mom was using some kind of remedy to wash me away. It feels real hot. . . . I know she is trying to get me out of her. I'm just a little blob. I don't know how I know, but I know. My aunt seems to be giving my mom directions. I can hear her voice and another woman in the background. My mother is not supposed to get pregnant. She doesn't know me. . . . It didn't work either. It had a strong harsh smell, almost a disinfectant smell, like ammonia, strong, a vile, strong smell. . . . I was way up there, just teeny. I knew nobody really wanted me . . . but I was determined. I was a fighter even then. . . . Poor Mom would die if she knew I knew all this stuff!"[42]

Fantasy? A metaphorical expression of actual feelings of being unwanted? This would be the most convenient explanation. And perhaps it does explain some of these memories. However, this mind-staggering abortion memory is no isolated case. Several amazing reports show that children remember attempted, but obviously failed, abortion procedures.[43]

Dee, a young woman, recalled a terrifying experience that occurred before her birth. She told Dr. Cheek that she was having a recurrent dream that her mother was trying to abort her with a button hook. Dr. Cheek explained that it would be almost impossible to get a button hook through the cervix. However, he hypnotized her with the possibility of verifying the unlikely event.

In Dee's words: "It's before I'm born. My father is shouting, 'I'm going to kill you!'" Pulling her legs up to her chest as if trying to escape from something frightening, Dee suddenly began screaming as she recalled this. Calming down, Dee continued: "I saw that button hook coming up at me. I knew my mother was trying to get me out."

"Then what?" prodded Dr. Cheek.

"Nothing—only a little bleeding."

"How do you know this?" asked Dr. Cheek.

"I know it the same way I have known other things about real people," Dee said, "and what is going to happen to them."

Several days later in a letter to Dr. Cheek, Dee's mother confirmed the fantastic story. Dee's father was a vicious alcoholic. He threatened to kill her mother if she did not abort Dee. She did indeed get out a button hook but could not complete the abortion.

"The panic that Dee had shown while recalling the button hook experience was, I believe," says Dr. Cheek, "a telepathic reflection of her mother's combined fear for her life and her anguish over the idea of destroying her child."[44]

In the course of his own primal therapy, Australian psychiatrist Graham Farrant recalled a similar disturbing event. He suddenly became convinced that his mother attempted to abort him. When he confronted his mother, she denied it. But Dr. Farrant's memory was hardly vague. He knew the details. He told his mother how she had taken pills and entered a hot tub. At that she broke into tears and cried, "You couldn't know this! I never told anybody."[45]

Canadian psychiatrist Josefine van Husen, M.D., has recorded some four dozen similar memories of abortion attempts.[46] Many of these were later confirmed by the mother who attempted the abortion. The memories first came to her attention when one of her clients in a hypnotic trance reacted with panic to the memory of being stuck in a dark chamber with mobile walls moving in and out.

"It finally struck me," recalls Dr. Van Husen, "that the only mobile, rhythmically contracting and enclosing walls I was familiar with as a physician were those of the womb.

"One day, while getting a detailed description of how the fearful person felt all curled up in a soft, dark corner trying to feel safe, I asked if she were aware of her body proportions. With that question being answered in the affirmative, I asked what was the size of the head in relation to the shoulders. When the answer was that the head was much bigger than the shoulders, it dawned on me that I must be listening to a prenatal recall.

"I then questioned how many months the person had been in that residence. I was told three months. Later checking my embryology text, which, I must admit, I was no longer too familiar with, I discovered the given head-shoulder dimension was accurate for the length of pregnancy." Dr. Van Husen has since used memory of body proportions as a guideline to the period of life recalled during the memory.

Recalling prenatal memories often facilitates emotional healing. For example, a twenty-seven-year-old M.A. in art and archaeology consulted Dr. Van Husen after disturbing childhood memories spontaneously erupted during her meditation. After much work with age regression techniques, she recalled multiple abortion attempts. Meanwhile her mother became strongly opposed to her daughter's seeking therapy. The visits stopped. Until one day the mother came to visit Dr. Van Husen. She had asked her daughter if she knew why she had attempted the abortion. The daughter said yes. Both in tears, the two women comforted each other and made peace.[47]

In the course of analyzing teenage attempted suicides, Canadian psychologist Andrew Feldmar uncovered an alarming relationship between abortion and later suicide attempts. Four of his patients had repeatedly attempted suicide at the same time of the year their mothers had attempted to abort them. Once they confronted the prenatal memory, the teenagers were free of the suicidal compulsion. More incredible, the children did not know, consciously or by any means of knowledge known to modern science, an abortion had been attempted.

A NEW LOOK AT MEMORY

Where does memory reside? What is the source and home of memory, of consciousness itself? Dr. Feldmar concludes: "The origin of consciousness, sentience, i.e., the beginning of one's relevant lifetime, must be dated at conception, if not before."[48]

The incredible detail of many prenatal memories, particularly memories of events outside the womb, suggests clairvoyance. But can one be clairvoyant before the brain is developed?

One of the most striking things about early prebirth memory is that the experiences remembered often occur before the brain and nervous system are formed. The further you go back in the womb, the more you run out of brain material to account for the memory, observes Dr. Chamberlain, until finally you are left with distinct memory, yet no brain at all. Moreover, the memories are not the thoughts and feelings of an immature, developing personality. They are mature, fully-formed thoughts, suggesting a mature, conscious entity.

For most people, the following tale transcends the limits of the credible. Ingrid recalls her mother and father, not yet married, making love on a couch—the lovemaking experience that led to her conception. The doorbell rang. Ingrid's grandmother and aunt had come back unexpectedly from shopping. The encounter sent shock waves through all present. Ingrid recalls: "Mother was beside herself. She knew she got pregnant. She was ashamed. She blamed me for her trouble."[49]

Ida also claims she recalls her own conception. Her parents were drunk and she felt the time was not right to go inside. She says she floated in a blissful place hard to describe, in swirls of light.[50]

Accounting for detailed memories of events occurring in the first trimester of intrauterine life means making a leap from science as we know it to the paranormal. It may even mean rethinking our knowledge of human memory and perhaps questioning whether memory is stored in the brain as most people believe.

Many people recall detailed and accurate events without benefit of either body or brain. These "out-of-body" experiences sometimes occur during surgery. For example cardiologist Michael Sabom published the detailed accounts of four patients who clearly viewed their own surgery while out of the body. In one case, a soldier with severe injuries from an explosion which blew out his eardrums and burned his eyes so he could not see for weeks, describes what he saw and heard while hovering over the battlefield and later over the operating table. He even identified the surgeon's voice, having heard it during surgery![51] For that matter, out-of-body memory seems to transcend the limitations of the physical senses. There is even a case on record of an anesthetized blind woman seeing vivid details including the doctor's clothing and shape and color of instruments used.[52]

Most medical scientists believe the brain is the seat of memory. Researchers have sought the mystery of memory for decades. Some scientists even feel that memory can be reduced to no more than a series of molecular events. But, as Dr. Chamberlain puts it, "the wonder of human memory will never be expressed by how much glucose is burned in the amygdala or how many neuropeptides have congregated in the hippocampus."[53] For that matter, *the idea that memory resides in the brain is a theory, not a fact.* No storehouse of memory in the brain has ever been found.

Surgery on animals has identified specific areas responsible for relaying certain types of memory from visual recognition memory to spatial memory. Surgically disconnecting certain areas of the brain such as the hippocampus and amygdala in the limbic system result in memory loss.[54] In a nutshell: If part of the brain is temporarily damaged, memory is lost. When that part of the brain is repaired, memory is regained. Voilà! Memory resides in the brain. Or so it would seem until you take another look at that reasoning. Dr. Chamberlain uses a television set as an analogy. Disconnect part of the TV set and programs cease coming through. Reconnect the part and the programs return. Who believes the programs are stored in the television set? But if memory is not stored in the brain, where is it stored?

In the 1960s some proposed the concept of cellular memory, based on the idea that memory may be stored in RNA "memory molecules" throughout the body. However, we now know that nerve cells and molecules are continually changing, renewing. So the RNA theory no longer seems probable. Could it be, as biologist Rupert Sheldrake suggests, that the brain, like a television set, is a tuning device and that memory storage is outside the brain—outside the body?[55]

Candace Pert, a pioneer in identifying neuropeptides, believes that the brain is the physical substrate of mind and memory, which has another "immaterial substrate."[56] In other words, the brain is an outward manifestation of the mind, but is not the mind. Dr. Chamberlain agrees. Since, during out-of-body experiences, damaged or even destroyed senses work well and anesthesia appears to have no effect on memory, it seems reasonable to propose, in his words, that "memory and other cognitive functions lie in a protected sphere outside the body."[57]

For that matter, telepathy and clairvoyance may also take place outside the body. After years of research and dozens of theories, no physical organ of extrasensory perception has ever been identified. The incredible stories of ESP during the childbearing season, which scientists have gathered and parents and children have remembered, suggests that perhaps a part of us—the mind, the soul, call it what you will—both predates birth and transcends death.

CHAPTER 6

Communicating With Your Unborn Child

Watch her unobserved and you may catch an expectant mother in a mood that reminds you of the soft glow of a greeting card. Her hand on her belly, her eyes cast down, a meditative look on her face, she almost seems to be telling secrets to her preborn child in a language beyond words.

She may be doing just that without realizing it.

Feelings are transmitted to the baby via the agency of hormones and other complex biochemical processes. And, as many childbirth professionals and parents have discovered, thoughts may also be conveyed on the wings of telepathy from the earliest minutes of pregnancy.

Throughout pregnancy, you can enhance your ability to communicate with your preborn child with a wide variety of exercises that include everything from guided imagery to games.

Transuterine communication—another name for communication between parent and preborn child—may yield a healthier, more rewarding pregnancy, a more fulfilling birth experience, and long-term benefits after the baby is born.

GETTING IN TOUCH WITH YOUR UNBORN CHILD

An inner journey into the womb is a powerful exercise you can use to heighten your intuition. During the exercise either or both parents imagine being face to face with the baby and then communicating with the unborn child. Childbirth educators have found many benefits of this exercise since I introduced this simple form of transuterine communication in my workshops for maternity health care professionals.

The instructions that follow are for both parents. Feel free to modify them to suit your own needs. This exercise can help you strengthen the lifelong family bond parents and child share; enhance preverbal communication with the baby; increase confidence in your ability to give birth safely; make effective birth plans; and make a smoother adjustment to parenthood.

COMMUNICATING WITH YOUR UNBORN CHILD

When you are settled down in a relaxed, comfortable position in a place where you won't be disturbed or distracted for the next fifteen minutes or so, take an inner journey to a very special place, the very center of your pregnancy: the womb.

Begin by breathing deeply and rhythmically, in through the nose and out either through the nose or through slightly parted lips, whichever you prefer. Become aware of your breathing. As you observe your breathing, let it become a little deeper, a little slower, without straining or forcing the breath in any way.

Now, imagine that each breath you take in is a soft, golden, radiant light. You can think of this light any way you want—perhaps as life energy or as a metaphor for the breath. Continue to breathe in this soft, golden light. Breathe this radiant light right into the center of your being. Let each breath you take in fill you more and more with this soft, golden, radiant light. And let each breath you expel relax you more and more. Each breath you expel melts tension away more and more.

Now, mothers: imagine that you are able to breathe this soft golden radiant light directly into your womb. With each breath in, radiant light fills your womb—the womb that is the center of your pregnancy, the center of all the changes taking place in your body, your emotions, your mind, all around you. Continue to breathe this radiant golden light into your womb until it surrounds your baby with its soft radiance.

Meanwhile, fathers: continue to breathe this radiant light into the very center of your being. And as you do, imagine that this light is somehow able to connect you, to link you, with your unborn child.

Now, both mothers and fathers, imagine that your mind, your consciousness, is somehow able to be in the womb with your baby and that you are face to face with your unborn child. Visualize the baby in any way that feels comfortable to you. You don't have to be concerned with how the baby actually appears at this state of development. Just picture the baby in whatever way feels right.

Perhaps you may want to imagine the baby lying head down surrounded by a crystal clear sea of amniotic fluid in his or her own private universe—perfectly comfortable, secure, at peace.

Enjoy being with your unborn child in this unique way for a little while. And as you do, if you find your attention wandering or if irrelevant thoughts come into your mind, gently bring your awareness back to your baby by mentally repeating the word *baby* with each breath you let out. "Baby . . . baby . . . baby." And let yourself go into an even deeper state of relaxation—body and mind.

Now, allow the love you feel for your child to well up within you.

At this point, you may want to talk with your baby. Tell your child anything you want: how you are feeling right now . . . how much you are looking forward to holding him or her in your arms . . . how much you love him or her . . . anything you want.

You may want to ask your baby a question: What do you most need right now? Where would you like to be born? What will you most need during the first week after birth? Ask any question you wish. Imagine that your baby can answer you—in words, images, impressions, by painting a picture in your mind's eye.

Don't be surprised if, while doing this exercise, you glimpse the baby's gender or some aspect of the baby's physical characteristics, even the baby's personality. This is perfectly normal. For now, dwell on the love you feel for your unborn child. And when you are ready to return to the world of everyday life, take a few deep breaths, stretch gently, count slowly to five, and open your eyes.

This exercise may spontaneously trigger your intuition. While doing the exercise, the expectant mother or father often glimpses the baby's gender, other physical characteristics, and even personality traits.

It is not necessary to believe your baby understands and responds to what you say. You may prefer to think of your dialogue with your unborn child as a metaphor for tapping your own inner wisdom. Some may feel that, during this exercise, the parents are connecting with their own unconscious feelings or thoughts rather than communicating with the baby.

Whether you believe this exercise triggers real communication with your unborn child or evokes your own intuition, it can be very helpful in tapping inner resources and resolving problems.

TAPPING YOUR INTUITION FOR A HEALTHIER PREGNANCY

You can use the previous excercise to help you enjoy a healthier pregnancy and more rewarding birth. Here are some suggestions:

> While doing the exercise, ask your baby a question such as: "What do I most need to do for a healthy pregnancy or healthy birth?" "How can I best meet your needs during this pregnancy?" or "Where would you like to be born?" Questions like these can assist you in clarifying your own feelings about these topics and to make more effective birth plans. Be creative. Ask whatever questions come to mind and are important to you.
>
> To enhance this exercise, trying playing relaxing music (no music with a heavy beat), eating a healthy well-balanced diet, curbing harmful substances (including sugar, alcohol, and caffeine), and getting plenty of rest.

While doing the exercise, you may get an impression of something in your diet the baby does not like. For instance, one New Jersey mother felt her child was disturbed when she had a cocktail.

Is this genuine parent-unborn communication? Or is the mother simply getting in touch with her own common sense? There is really no way to tell. Realizing that immoderate quantities of alcohol are harmful to the growing baby hardly requires an encounter with paranormal communication. Feeling the baby's reaction to the alcohol, on the other hand, may. The important point is that the mother *felt* the communication took place, "just with thoughts, but it was very real. I felt I was really tuned into it."

THE VARIETIES OF TRANSUTERINE COMMUNICATION

Parent-preborn communication occasionally takes the form of a vision, fantasy, or waking dream. Utah midwife, Laurine Kingston, recalls an unusual event that almost seems like a gift from the unborn child. "Ginger, one of my clients, had been terrified of death throughout her pregnancy since her own mother had recently died of cancer," reports Laurine. "One afternoon while washing the dishes, Ginger suddenly sensed something most peculiar. It was as if her own child, unborn and still in the womb, was somehow standing near her. Ginger felt her child was reassuring her, telling her in nonverbal language that everything was going to be all right. When Ginger shared this experience with me, crying, I felt almost as if we were encapsuled in a pastel glow. I had goose bumps all over. Both of us sensed that everything would be all right. There was no question that this was not just a fantasy."

But if it was not fantasy, what was it? Does this episode fall into the category of parent-child telepathy? Or could the episode be explained in terms of the mother's intuition, appearing as communication with the unborn? Or, is it just fantasy after all? We may never be able to answer these questions. But whatever the explanation, Ginger is not the only expectant parent to report feeling that she has received distinct messages from her still developing child.

Kristi Ridd, childbirth companion coordinator for the state of Utah, reports a sense of maternal-unborn communication that had a dramatic effect on the labor of one of her client's.

Carrie, a mother of two, was a victim of sexual abuse. Unresolved trauma of this sort often comes to mind during labor, creating emotional tension that can trigger complications in childbirth such as prolonged labor. Carrie's first two births ended with the need for epidural anesthesia and forceps delivery because labor stopped during the birth process.

During her third pregnancy, Carrie elected for a home birth to decrease the chance of complications resulting from tension in an unfamiliar environment. Her labor progressed normally until second stage (the birth process) when contractions suddenly stopped.

Carrie recalls feeling out of touch with her body even after two hours of hard pushing without progress. She could not seem to feel involved with her child, or the birth process, painful as it was becoming after hours without progress.

Kristi and the attending midwife knew that for the safety of the baby, Carrie should soon be transferred to the hospital unless her labor progressed. As a last resort, however, before transporting the mother, Kristi suggested Carrie center her mind inward and get in touch with her unborn child.

When Carrie imagined her child within, something inexplicable occurred. Carrie felt as if the baby were talking to her.

"I'm going to be born," the baby seemed to say in a language beyond words. "And I'm going to help you!"

There is no logical explanation for an experience like this; there is not even an illogical one. Yet getting in touch with her unborn child altered the course of Carrie's labor. Dramatically. Immediately. Within minutes after feeling she had made contact with her unborn baby, her child was born.

Fantasy? The mother's own intuition couched in the language of the unborn? Or is it? In the face of all reason which tells us it can't happen, it never happens, it's impossible, the inexplicable continues to occur. People who have such experiences—and those who have witnessed the results of parent-unborn communication again and again in their health care practice—are sometimes tempted to believe that the unborn child is really trying to communicate.

One twenty-three year old who vividly remembers the experience of being born has this to say about the time immediately after birth: "Mom's still crying a little bit but not like before. I knew I was okay. I tried to tell everybody, but they wouldn't listen."[1]

Perhaps it's time we listened.

GETTING TO KNOW YOUR UNBORN CHILD

The Basque people take part in one of the most beautiful childbearing rituals known to any culture. During pregnancy, the expectant parents tell one another stories about the baby with the belief that the child in utero can hear the tales. They also sing to their child. The songs they sing are later repeated during birth and after the baby is born. During birth, the family forms concentric circles around the mother, father, and sibling. They sing, chant, and play music to cheer the laboring mother, "massaging the mother and baby with laughter."[2]

PLAYING WITH YOUR UNBORN CHILD

The following may enhance the sense of communication you share with your preborn child as it helps you to adjust to your new role as parent:

- Feel the baby gently through the abdominal and uterine walls. See if you can identify the baby's position in utero. Where is the head? The back? The arms? The legs?
- Play music to your child or sing a relaxing lullaby
- Talk with your baby in a soft calming voice; to best be heard in utero, the expectant father can speak close to the mother's abdomen (odd as it may appear to an onlooker!)

Your family may also enjoy some of these preborn activities.

If you palpate the baby through the abdominal and uterine walls, do it gently but firmly. See if you can feel the baby's outline. Identifying the baby's position in utero is not quite as easy as it sounds! Don't worry if you cannot correctly tell one part of the baby from the other! This is a skill that comes with much practice, and even the practiced are sometimes inaccurate. Experienced maternity care professionals with sensitive hands occasionally fail to identify head from buttocks. Some have been surprised to discover a buttocks first (breech) at birth when they had thought the baby was in a vertex (head down) position! The baby's position varies widely and changes from time to time throughout pregnancy. In addition, the placenta is often on the front uterine wall. All of this explains why palpation is erratic at best.

Since your preborn baby hears the music you play, the songs you sing, and even the stories you tell, you may want to try talking with your baby. Do not feel these games should be a learning experience for your baby. The meaning of the words you speak is less important than the feelings you convey.

You may also want to experiment with different forms of music and keep track of the baby's movements to see how your child reacts. The purpose is not educating your child to recognize the difference between Clementi and Corelli but exposing your child to the world of beautiful music. Some parents have found that if a particular piece of music is played during the prenatal period at the end of a "communication session," the same music will be useful in decreasing the baby's activity level and helping it to sleep if played after it is born.[3]

PRENATAL GAMES

Throughout his wife's pregnancy, a Canadian father pressed his face on his mate's abdomen and said "Hoo, hoo!" each night. During the twenty-fifth week of pregnancy, the unexpected occurred. The father felt pressure against his cheek. He pulled his face away to see a bulge on the abdominal wall. He then pressed his face against the other side of the abdomen and repeated his greeting. The bulge moved to that side. Clearly, the baby was playing tag.[4] They played the game throughout pregnancy. And the father repeated the game with similar results during the next pregnancy. Early during the second pregnancy, an ultrasound scan was done. When the technician was unable to stimulate the then *one-inch long embryo* to change position in utero for better viewing, the father uttered his greeting. The embryo moved in response![5]

During birth, the obstetrician used forceps to complete a prolonged labor. The exhausted newborn was at his mother's breast nursing when the father once again uttered his greeting. To the amazement of the attending physician the newborn stopped nursing and turned around to search for the source of the familiar sound!

Another expectant father talked to his developing baby regularly through the third trimester of pregnancy. He cupped his hand over his mate's abdomen and spoke a few times each week. After the baby was born in a rather noisy hospital setting with several people talking at once, the father, facing his child's back, whispered to him. The newborn immediately turned around and faced his dad. Clearly, he recognized and appreciated this voice.

Prenatal games frequently trigger intuitive episodes. "During my first pregnancy," recalls Naia, a new mother, "my husband, John, had an intuitive experience with our unborn son. One night while lying in bed, John reached over and put his hand on my abdomen. Looking startled, he pulled his hand away quickly. He said that he had been concentrating on our child who we already intuited was a boy and named Nick. When he put his hand on my abdomen, Nick suddenly moved. John was surprised and said that he sensed what Nick looked like at that time. After Nick was born, the medical staff put him on a warming tray, since he was born by c-section. When John came in to see us, Nick reached up and pulled John's hand down onto his face."

A few expectant parents try preborn games with their unborn child by gently poking the abdominal wall and seeing whether or not the baby responds. Many babies do learn to respond to a gentle physical stimulus. To enhance the experience, talk to your baby also.

Obstetrician Rene Van de Carr developed an organized program of playing with and stimulating the unborn child. When Dr. Van De Carr developed his program in the 1970s, he was running a busy medical practice and was chief of obstetrics at St. Rose Hospital in Hayward, California. Like many parents and professionals who pay attention to newborns, he observed that babies born to mothers who used no medications during labor were more alert and more "personlike."[6] Unlike most of his colleagues, he believed that preborn babies were far more aware during pregnancy than medical science realized. He wondered if there could be valuable social and emotional consequences of interacting with the parents while the unborn's sensory systems were being developed. He sought answers from medical professionals and written research. And, like many pioneers in a new field, he came up with dead ends. Obstetricians had not come to believe babies had much ability before birth. Psychologists thought the idea was ridiculous.[7] So Dr. Van de Carr created his own program of prenatal stimulation and called it Prenatal University. In essence, the suggestions he has taught to over a thousand expectant couples involve encouraging parents to communicate with, sing to, and love the baby before the child is born.

Like the exercise called "Getting in Touch With Your Unborn Child," Van de Carr's suggestions help the mother, father, and sibling come to accept and relate to their child as an individual before birth and recognize that the growing child, still unseen, is an understanding and responsive being. Though every family can benefit from spending time with the unborn, extra attention to the unborn child may be particularly useful for populations identified as high risk for child abuse. According to Van de Carr, "It is easier for the parents to create positive role behaviors for a baby before it is born."[8] Siblings, too, can benefit from these simple exercises. Sibling rivalry is likely to be markedly reduced as the sibling-to-be feels an active participant in pregnancy and prenatal baby care.

Dr. Van de Carr says babies who experience his program are often born with eyes open at the instant of birth, are more alert, more easily calmed by patting, rubbing, or music, and cry less. They also turn more quickly toward the sound of a voice and can concentrate for longer periods at a time.

Do the exercise as often as you like. Dr. Van de Carr suggests trying these activities for about five minutes twice daily during the last three or four months of pregnancy. Some parents, however, may prefer a weekly session.

Since babies develop regular sleep patterns in utero, the exercises are likely to be most effective when the baby is moving. Dr. Van de Carr suggests tailoring parent-unborn activities to the baby's growth in utero.

Beginning at about the fifth month of pregnancy, you might want to try the "kick game." Press into the abdominal wall gently and see if the baby responds with a kick. Some parents are surprised to find that the baby responds by kicking the same number of times the mother or father presses! Other expectant parents have found that as they moved their hand to different areas of the abdomen, the baby followed and moved its foot.

"As you can imagine," says Van de Carr, "this is a quite convincing demonstration to the parents that their baby is responding to them and is already a little human being."[9]

However, do not depend on dramatic results. Not all preborn children follow the same rules in playing games!

By around the eighth month, you can try story or Bible reading, playing symphonic music and opera.

BOY OR GIRL? TESTS AND FOLKLORE

The following story was reported by a pharmacist. An excited man came into the pharmacy to purchase prenatal vitamins for his wife who was pregnant with their first child after years of trying. During conversation, the happy dad-to-be told the pharmacist how much he hoped for a boy. When the pharmacist gave the man his wife's vitamins, which happened to be pink-and-blue capsules, he joked: "If you want a boy, be sure to have your wife swallow the blue end first." The man left the pharmacy. Apparently he didn't realize the pharmacist was joking, for two hours later, he returned and asked: "Which end did you say to swallow first for a boy?"

As most less-naive parents realize, there is really nothing you can do to change the gender of your child once the child is growing in utero. However, there is a wealth of folklore about getting an advance glimpse of your child's gender. More than two thousand years ago, the ancient Greeks had a unique method of finding out whether the expectant mother was carrying a boy or a girl. Someone would place a sprig of parsley on her head without her knowing it. The very next person she spoke to would be the same sex as her baby. So goes the legend. The Medieval English had a lovely custom. Someone offered the expectant mother a choice of lily or rose; if she selected the lily, the child was a boy; the rose, a girl.

There are a number of modern versions of the boy-girl test. If the fetal heartbeat is fast, the baby will be a girl; if slow, a boy; if you're carrying high, a girl, low, a boy; if the baby is a vigorous kicker, a boy, and so on. Though often quoted, these are unreliable diagnostics. However, there is another tool some parents have found effective.

Hypnosis experts use a method called the Chevroux pendulum technique to tune into your intuition.[10]

For some, this method works wonderfully. One study that physician Mike Samuels mentions claims the method was more than 90 percent accurate about the unborn baby's gender for those who got a definite yes or no answer in the third trimester.[11] (Ninety percent is nothing less than astounding considering that the law of averages would give a 50 percent correct answer. However, the Samuels results do not indicate the size of the population involved in the study.)

BOY OR GIRL EXERCISE

Take a one-foot piece of thread or string with a small weight (such as a ring) attached to one end. Hold the cord lightly between thumb and forefinger while asking yourself a simple question to which the answer is yes, such as, "Am I pregnant?" The pendulum may begin to move in one direction. (This doesn't work for everyone.)

Now ask a question to which the answer is no. The pendulum may begin to move in another direction.

Finally, ask yourself another questions with an "I don't know" answer. The pendulum may make a third and different motion.

Once you are familiar with the motions that correspond to each answer, ask the pendulum "Is my unborn child a boy?" If this method works for you, the pendulum will swing in the motion associated with boy or girl.

For those who don't get definite pendulum movements for yes, no, and maybe, the method is about unreliable.

My wife, Jan, and I tried this technique ourselves. When we asked the pendulum if the baby was a boy, it said yes. When we asked if the baby was a girl, it also said yes. The dramatic result would be having twins, one boy and one girl—practically incontrovertible evidence of a paranormal phenomenon. However, our child was a boy. So much for pendulums.

SUMMING UP

Scientific research is just beginning to reveal a fact about human babies that nearly every midwife, every mother, and certainly every baby knows intuitively.

Health professionals have observed the same phenomenon again and again. Babies who are nurtured through pregnancy and born in an emotionally positive climate into loving hands, begin life in the best possible way. You can see it in their eyes, their facial expressions, their gestures. They gaze around at their new world with fascination, taking it all in. They act secure, at peace, and make an intense bond with their parents with eye-to-eye contact and touch.[12]

The thoughts and feelings you communicate reach your preborn child. Reaching your baby now during pregnancy and communicating feelings of love may mean a healthier, happier child. By focusing love and positive energy into the womb—baby's private universe—you may be able to create a healthier pregnancy, shape your baby's birth, and perhaps, by so doing, even change the world.

CHAPTER 7

EXPECTANT PARENTS' DREAMS: DOORWAY TO THE EXTRAORDINARY

While pregnant with her first child, Amy, a woman living in a suburb of Denver, Colorado, had a remarkable dream. Prior to the dream, she and her husband, Arthur, both felt the baby was a girl. During an ultrasound scan, the technician was unable to spot a penis, which confirmed the parents' feelings about the baby's gender. So Arthur and Amy began to think of girls' names. Until the night of Amy's unforgettable dream.

Two or three weeks before the birth, Amy dreamed she was floating down a beautiful clear river in the fall. It was very peaceful and calm, with just the hint of a current. Autumn leaves were drifting slowly to the water. In the dream she was in a canoe. Sitting in front of her, facing her, was a little blond boy about ten years old. The boy introduced himself as Jonathan and said he was her soon-to-be son. They had a long conversation concerning their relationship with each other, past, present, and future. After the dream, Amy and Arthur decided to name their child Jonathan, feeling that the baby was a boy, despite the ultrasound. Jonathan is now ten years old, very blond and blue eyed. Despite Amy's dark Mediterranean coloring, the boy took after his father's side of the family.

Jonathan is the very image, recalls Amy, of the child she spoke with in her dream.

THE CHANGING DREAM WORLD OF EXPECTANT PARENTS

During the early stages of sleep, brain activity slows down. Breathing and heartbeat also become slower. Then, after a period of rest, REM sleep occurs. REM sleep takes its name from rapid eye movements occurring under closed (or partially closed) lids. This phase of sleep is associated with dreaming activity. In REM sleep, respiration is higher and irregular. Oxygen consumption increases. Systolic blood pressure is higher and shows greater fluctuations. Body movements usually lead to a change of position while facial movements are meaningful and typical of those seen in the waking state. Everyone experiences REM sleep and dreaming. However, for most parents, pregnancy opens the door on richer, more vivid dreams. As Sue, a mother in Montana, recalls: "I had many more dreams when I was pregnant. They were very vivid—more so than before I was pregnant."

COMMON DREAM THEMES IN EXPECTANT MOTHERS

Among many other topics, expectant mothers typically dream about

- Reliving their childhood
- Reliving their school days
- Conflicts between career and motherhood
- Mothering skills
- Feeding the baby

The expectant mother's dreams are frequently strikingly different from the dreams of the nonpregnant person. There are many possible reasons for this. One is that universal scapegoat: hormonal changes, though there is no proof hormonal changes initiate a fraction of the emotional transformations for which they are credited (or blamed, however one wants to look at it). The need to urinate frequently and a more awkward sleeping position as the mother's abdomen grows may also alter the mother's sleep patterns, perhaps causing her to dream more. Yet another possible reason is the fact that pregnancy is a life crisis, eliciting apprehensions nearly all parents-to-be face.

Medical research has shown that dreaming may be a major form of preparation for motherhood. As one would expect, the dream content of expectant mothers parallels their waking concerns. Women tend to have five major categories of dreams: reliving childhood, school dreams, motherhood-career conflicts, confidence in maternal skills, and food-infant interaction.[1]

COMMON DREAM THEMES IN EXPECTANT FATHERS

Among many other topics, expectant fathers often dream about

- Their own father
- Their mate's changes
- Being pregnant
- Giving birth
- Fathering skills

Expectant fathers also experience the dream world of pregnancy. Like the mother's dreams, the father's dream life often follows pregnancy's progression. First trimester dreams sometimes reflect wishes to be creative like their partner. The expectant father's second trimester dreams sometimes include images of physical changes about the mother, and even dreams of being pregnant himself. Some men report giving birth in innovative ways, including the baby coming through the navel, and even out the ears. Third trimester dreams frequently project scenes as a father with a newborn or older child.[2]

DREAM SYMBOLS

Dream symbols are images or pictures in a dream that usually stand for a thought, feeling, condition, event, person, or place in the dreamer's life. There is no final interpretation of any dream.[3] The meaning behind each dream depends on the individual. For this reason, we can't assign a single meaning to any particular symbol. However, certain symbols typically recur during pregnancy dreams. These often, but not always, signify similar themes. A few common pregnancy dream motifs are outlined on page 88.[4]

Expectant fathers often have dream symbols similar to the mother's. In addition, the father may dream of being abandoned or left out, or he may have dreams about competition and rivalry. These often reflect his very common concerns about being displaced by the child.[5] One expectant father's dream is both humorous and sad. "I am at a baseball game," he recalls of his dream. "I get up to go get some beer. When I return, I can't find my seat. I look for a new one but while the stadium is not full, many of the women are pregnant and taking up two seats."[6]

PREGNANCY DREAM SYMBOLS AND WHAT THEY MAY MEAN

- Small animals and sometimes even plants may symbolize the growing child in early pregnancy.
- Large plants and animals, as one might expect, may represent the baby in late pregnancy.
- Shopping for clothing, going on a journey, or even a catastrophe, may denote the transition to motherhood.
- Rooms, houses, buildings, and other architectural structures may symbolize the womb, which is, after all, baby's temporary home.
- Images of water, both lakes and turbulent oceans, symbolize the birth process itself.

Dreams of vessels—from caves to washing machines—often symbolize the womb for the expectant father as well as for the mother. One father dreamed: "My wife and I are at an amusement park full of household items that are giant sized. We are riding a giant washing machine agitator. My wife is trying to hang on. She laughs and says she used to do this as a child. I look at her and see she has in fact become a small child."[7]

Bear in mind that these dream symbols, common as they are to many expectant parents, do not apply to all. Dreaming of going on a journey, for example, may very well connote the passage rite of becoming a parent. Or it may simply signify a vacation you would like to plan. To determine the meaning of a dream symbol, ask yourself what this reminds you of in your waking life.

When examining a dream, look for the first interpretation of a symbol that comes to mind. More often than not, this is the most meaningful one.[8] Dream experts agree that your own personal association about a dream image is the only way to uncover its true meaning. If the meaning for the image doesn't feel right, reject it and try another.[9]

Often the rich symbolic language of dreams veils a hidden meaning—knowledge that the mother may have acquired through unconscious perception of subliminal impressions or perhaps even paranormal awareness.

During her second pregnancy, Kim, a North Carolina mother, experienced a highly symbolic dream giving her accurate information about her unborn child.

"I had a dream the night my son (now two years old) Nicholas was conceived," she recalls. "The dream was very vivid and had a weird feel to it. It was about a puppy. For some reason I had found this puppy nearly drowned in a bucket of cleaning water in my mother-in-law's house. Everyone was very upset about it, but I forced myself to remain calm and applied what little I knew of animal artificial respiration! The puppy coughed up a splotch of thin brownish fluid and began to breathe again, and everyone was very pleased. It was a cute, fuzzy little boy puppy.

"I vividly remembered the dream the next morning, and thought it wasn't at all like normal dreams. About a week later, a few days before my period was due, I had a strange brownish discharge that was the color and almost the exact shape of the splotch of fluid the puppy had coughed up in the dream! And, that was all that I had for a period that month.

"Later when tests confirmed pregnancy, I was concerned that the earlier discharge had been a sign of some sort of problem with the baby. But I made up my mind to think positive thoughts and have a healthy baby! I also knew, from the dream, that my baby was a boy. I never tried to think of girls' names, and when stocking the nursery I didn't hesitate to buy boys' stuff."

Kim's child was indeed the healthy boy she had dreamed of.

NIGHTMARES

Most mothers have nightmares reflecting their concerns and fears about their developing child. Most of the these dreams are just that: dreams. Disturbing dreams are common during pregnancy, reflecting worries most expectant parents share about the developing child. In fact, pregnant women frequently have more nightmares, reflecting their anxieties

---

COMMON THEMES IN NIGHTMARES

- Fear the baby will be deformed or die
- Fear of being an inadequate parent
- Anxiety about losing one's mate
- Concern about having a difficult birth
- Concern about loss of control over the body, the mind, and emotions as the pregnancy or labor seems to take over
- Concerns about finances

More often than not, these dreams are no cause for concern. However, if the dreams persist or you feel they are more than mere nightmares, consult your health care provider.

---

and concerns, than pleasant dreams.[10] *This is a perfectly normal part of pregnancy and usually no reason for concern.*

Most expectant parents have many of the same fears regarding their developing child's well-being and their own changing lives. For example, Alicia, a thirty-two-year-old journalist had this dream: "The doctors looked doubtful . . . told me the newborn might not live . . . then she flopped over and died."[11] An eighteen-year-old mother dreamed her baby had a face like an old man's, with fangs coming out his mouth.[12] Both these mothers gave birth to normal, healthy children, as do most mothers who experience terrible nightmares.

Another expectant mother, who already had young children, dreamed that her apartment was invaded with all sorts of little animals, from rabbits to lizards, coming in the windows, through the front door, and messing up everything.[13] Since young animals in pregnancy dreams usually (but not always) symbolize the developing baby, the mother-to-be who dreamed her home was being taken over was probably justifiably concerned about the change yet another child would bring.

Toward late pregnancy, women frequently dream realistically or symbolically of a difficult birth. One mother dreamed she was climbing over a rocky chasm with rushing tides and crocodiles waiting. The water probably symbolized labor, and menacing animals typically symbolize the emerging child.[14]

ALTERING YOUR DREAMS

If you have recurrent nightmares, you may want to try to change the ending of the dream. You can do this in the following ways:

- Keep the dream image in mind as you drift back to sleep. However, this time, rewrite the script. Think of how you would like the disturbing dream to end and keep this image in mind.
- Try rewriting the dream while you are wide awake. Imagine yourself dreaming the same dream and giving it a different ending.

REWRITING DISTURBING DREAMS

A tribe in Malaysia called the Senoi have a wonderful way of handling children's nightmares. They ask the dreamer to attempt to redream the nightmare and recreate the scene.[15] You can try the same thing. If you have recurrent disturbing dreams, you may want to make the dream part of a simple self-created fantasy and rewrite the scene.

EXTRASENSORY DREAMS

Briana, a first-time mother living in New Jersey, woke terrified from a vivid nightmare that had a strangely real quality different from normal dreams. She dreamed her baby was being strangled by a snake. Terrified, she consulted her physician to see if the baby was healthy. An ultrasound revealed that the baby was, in fact, being asphyxiated by the umbilical cord. An emergency cesarean was immediately performed. Paying attention to her intuitive dream saved her child's life.

Leah, a teacher and mother in Louisiana, describes another vivid example of a clairvoyant dream. "During my pregnancy I had the most vivid dreams I've ever had in my life. Some of the dreams were just entertaining—like watching a movie, but others were clairvoyant. Though I never had a dream about my own child, I dreamed accurately about other people. "In one dream, another teacher came up to me at lunch and said, 'Guess what! I'm six weeks pregnant!' The next day at lunch I saw the woman and called her over and told her about my dream. She got the strangest expression on her face and asked me if I had been talking to her husband. I told her that I didn't even know her husband. It turned out that she was six weeks pregnant and hadn't told anyone except her husband."

No one has yet done a study to determine if paranormal dreams are more common during pregnancy than at other times. However, after completing a prolonged study of thousands of pregnancy dreams, clinical psychologist and dream expert Patricia Maybruck, Ph.D., was amazed to find that many of the dreams she had gathered correctly revealed information about conditions and events such as developing problems in the baby that were either presently occurring or were to occur in the future.

INTUITIVE DREAMS OF PREGNANCY

During the prenatal months, the expectant mother, father, and others close to the family may have several types of intuitive dreams.

These include the following:

- *Announcing dreams* revealing information about the baby.
- *Naming dreams*, during which the baby seems to be communicating with the parents and usually says his or her name
- *Prodromal dreams*, revealing information about current conditions and usually based on subliminal perceptions
- *Precognitive dreams*, announcing ESP-perceived future events

---

Often, however, what may seem extrasensory at first glance is simply coincidence. For example, Mara, a woman living in Toronto who has never been pregnant, had a series of dreams about pregnant friends that probably can be explained in terms of her empathizing with the women rather than in terms of intuition. "My dreams relating to pregnancy were more like images just before waking. When a cousin was pregnant with her first child, I saw myself pregnant and having labor contractions. I felt nothing. I woke up slightly panicky because I was frightened at the thought of being pregnant, not having any such plans myself. Sure enough, on waking I discovered that I was not pregnant, but the family informed me two days later that my cousin had had a baby boy on the day of my dream.

"With my sister, I knew she was going to be induced because she was overdue. My dream consisted of her telling me that she had had a cesarean. As it turned out, she did have a cesarean because the cord was wrapped around the baby's neck."

Occasionally the expectant mother or father will have a dream capturing the awe, magic, and mystery of pregnancy, reflecting what may be a transpersonal awareness. "I spent the day pruning," one father recalls of his dream during the first trimester. "It is miraculous. She is growing and changing just like the buds." The dreamer felt tiny compared to the vast process he was witnessing. He says: "Why was I small? I was witnessing something much larger, cosmic. Watching the large growth and I was part of it."[16]

Intuitive pregnancy dreams are so common they fall into several distinct categories we can call *announcing dreams*, *naming dreams*, *prodromal dreams*, and *precognitive dreams*.

ANNOUNCING DREAMS

Unique to pregnancy, the *announcing dream* reveals information about the baby beyond the parents' knowledge. It is almost as if the baby, preparing for the passage rite of birth, were to announce his or her arrival. The announcing dream typically reveals the baby's gender, one or more physical characteristics, and sometimes personality traits.

Sheryl, a Michigan nurse, recalls a dream she had on March 4, 1993. She says: "I was having an ultrasound scan when the office nurse peeked her head in the door and told the ultrasound technician that I wanted to know what sex the baby was if we could find out. The ultrasound tech turned around from looking at the nurse and said 'You want me to tell what she already knows: It's a boy!' On March 18, an actual ultrasound scan was done and confirmed the dream."

Dr. Ian Stevenson, professor of psychiatry and director of the Division of Personality Studies in the Department of Behavioral Medicine and Psychiatry at the University of Virginia, has investigated among the Tlingit Indians of southeastern Alaska twenty-nine apparent announcing dreams occurring before birth. "The dreamer correctly stated the sex of the baby in twenty-six cases," he reports. "This score of correct hits is far above the chance expectation of fourteen for the series and strongly suggests some paranormal capacity in these women for predicting the sex of unborn babies."[17]

Announcing dreams most frequently occur during the latter months of pregnancy, though there are exceptions that seem to be related to individual cultures. For example, in Burma, where people believe in reincarnation, the dreams almost invariably occur before conception, whereas among the Tlingit Indians, they usually occur just before birth.

Relatives and friends of expectant parents often have announcing dreams, which makes these characteristic dreams even more mysterious. Samantha, a working mother in Texas, dreamed about a coworker's unborn child. "While I was six months pregnant with my daughter Sue, a friend and coworker, Melissa, had been trying to get pregnant for several years with no success. I dreamed I saw Melissa walking toward the building where I worked. She was carrying a boy toddler.

"I told her about this dream. Later, she told me she was pregnant. She gave birth to a boy."

Inexplicable as they are, announcing dreams are among the most common types of intuitive dream during the prenatal months. The term, *announcing dream*, is borrowed from Dr. Stevenson's reincarnation research. People who believe in reincarnation feel the announcing dream arises from a deceased person who announces his or her imminent (re)birth either to the pregnant woman, her husband, family, or friends.[18] The incarnating personality sometimes purportedly gives information about his or her physical characteristics or even personality.

However, this fascinating dream type is by no means limited to people who believe in reincarnation. Another researcher, Ian Wilson, offers an alternative hypothesis to explain reincarnation dreams and memories. He suggests that the mother's dreams and mental traumas might be transmitted to the unborn child.[19]

Dr. Stevenson has probably done more research in the arena of reincarnation than any parapsychologist. In the course of thirty-five years in parapsychology, he has documented some 600 cases of paranormal memory worldwide. Many of these paranormal episodes occurred during pregnancy in the form of announcing dreams and revealed information about the unborn child to the parents or their relatives.

For example, an expectant mother of the Tlingit Indians dreamed her great-grandmother was visiting her and seated at a table. She said she was coming to stay with the dreamer. When the mother woke, she told her husband they were going to have a girl. Later, a girl was born.[20]

While studying the Gitskan Indians of British Columbia, anthropologist Antonia Mills reports another announcing dream that is cast in the background of reincarnation belief. Margaret flew to Vancouver to attend the birth of her daughter's first child. "On the eve of the baby's birth," writes Dr. Mills, "Margaret dreamed of her [deceased] mother so vividly that she said, 'Mother, what are you doing in Vancouver?' From the dream Margaret knew her mother was returning, and she said to her son-in-law, 'Don't count on a boy. Mother was here.' "[21]

The baby was indeed a girl and was accepted as the reincarnated great-grandmother.

Like all forms of intuition, paranormal dreams are most likely to occur in cultures or among people who accept and expect this sort of phenomenon. Cultural belief, Dr. Stevenson finds, influences the number of reported cases of reincarnation dreams. Cultures that believe in reincarnation report a higher percentage of extrasensory dreams giving accurate information about the baby couched in the language of reincarnation.

Announcing dreams are part of the cultural expectations of the Tlingit Indians and are likely to be remembered. The Tlingits believe in reincarnation and feel their announcing dreams give information about the identity of a person returning to terrestrial life. They have perhaps the highest percentage of reported reincarnation cases of any culture in the world.[22]

Of the 600 cases in Stevenson's files, almost half come from areas such as northern India, Burma, and Thailand, where reincarnation is part of the cultural belief.[23]

Announcing dreams often include a striking element we can call the *revealing motif*. This is the vehicle or symbol in the dream that imparts knowledge of the unborn child's characteristics. For example, in Sheryl's dream, an ultrasound technician revealed the baby's gender.

Revealing motifs are woven into dreams in a wide variety of forms. Common motifs include dreaming that the abdominal wall suddenly becomes as clear as glass and that the mother can see through it, the announcement of a nurse or other health professional relating the information either in words or by taking some action such as removing the baby's diaper and showing the mother the gender, seeing the baby through the window of a nursery, receiving a letter or card in the mail, even receiving a computer printout about the future child.

Carol Ann, an engineer from Cleveland, Ohio, has never been pregnant herself, yet she has had probable announcing dreams along with other intuitive experiences revealing the gender of friends' unborn babies. Her intuition has proven accurate even when the mother has been convinced otherwise.

"I had a dream that felt like one I should pay attention to," Carol Ann recalls. "In the dream, I was with the mother, and a lump like the baby's head with a distinct outline of a bow on it protruded from her belly! Though the mother thought her child was a boy, the bow symbol indicated to me she was a girl. The child was a girl.

"Another time when my husband's sister was pregnant, I was falling asleep and while in a very relaxed state, I had an overwhelming feeling that her baby would be a girl. It was her fourth child. She had previously had two girls and a boy and really hoped it would be a boy. I told my husband it would be a girl which it was."

Carol Ann had another probable announcing dream with a revealing motif about a friend's unborn twins in Sweden. "In the dream," Carol Ann recalls, "I have my hand on her belly and can feel the baby on top. It's definitely a girl in my dream. I'm not feeling anatomy, I'm just getting an impression from the contact. I have a stronger feeling from the baby on top. I couldn't tell the gender of the other twin in my dream, but sensed she was a girl.

"I told the parents I thought their twins were both girls."

The twins were, indeed, both girls.

In this dream, the *revealing motif* is the hand on the belly—a typical revealing motif, especially common in midwives who do abdominal palpation in the course of their practice.

Like many who have regular intuitive experiences, Carol Ann seems to specialize in intuitive dreams of pregnancy. She also dreamed of a woman who works in another division of her company. "I hadn't known she was pregnant or even trying," Carol Ann recalls. "In my dream, I see her walk by out of the side of my eye and notice that she looks quite pregnant. I say to the person I'm with in the dream that I didn't even know Alice was pregnant! A couple days later, I met Alice at the party of a mutual friend. As we were leaving the party, Alice mentioned that she was pregnant!"

On yet another occasion, Carol Ann tried deliberately to evoke her intuition regarding the gender of a pregnant coworker's child. "It was the mother's first baby and she thought it was a girl," recalls Carol Ann. "Several times, I put myself into a relaxed state and thought about the family. Each time, it felt like the child would be a boy. This proved true."

Another mother, Angelia from Missouri, had a nightmare that may be an announcing dream, though there is no specific revealing motif. The nightmare was cast in the setting of a science fiction novel she had read in which defective babies were shredded, and hence called "shredders." In one scene of this very detailed dream, Angelia recalls: "I received the bad news. My daughter was a shredder, an unfit baby, because of her heart and she had been disposed of. I screamed as if I would not stop.

REVEALING MOTIFS

Paranormal dreams revealing the baby's gender typically include an element I call the *revealing motif*. The dreamer's personality probably shapes this motif as it does all dream images. Typical revealing motifs include the following:

- Seeing through the abdominal wall
- Seeing the baby through a nursery window
- A nurse showing the baby's gender
- An ultrasound scan
- Receiving a card, letter, or computer printout with the baby's gender

---

"I awoke in my own bed, sitting bolt upright.

"The baby came two months later," Angelia reports. "Alexandra seemed perfect. But at her six-week check up, the doctor said he heard a heart murmur. He diagnosed an atrial septal defect.

"The cardiologist confirmed the diagnoses with an ultrasound. My baby was indeed a 'shredder,' according to the terms of the science fiction.

"Today Alex is fifteen months old and has outgrown her problem. She is happy, healthy, growing like a weed, and into everything in her reach. My precognition? Just the Irish coming out, as my mother would say."

Often the baby is older in the announcing dream, a toddler, a preadolescent, or even a young adult. The *older child motif* is another common characteristic of many pregnant dreams revealing information about the unborn child. During these dreams, the unborn child often appears older—from toddler to adult. In the dream, the dreamer (who may be mother, father, family member, or friend) often sees the child's gender, physical characteristics, such as eye or hair color, or even personality traits. Often the child appears to be speaking to the dreamer. *It is almost as if the dreamer were communicating with the spirit of the unborn.*

Patti, a systems programmer for a major New York university, reports a dream in which her unborn child appeared as an older child. "When I was pregnant with my eldest daughter," Patti recalls, "my husband and I had been together for four years and he had told me from the start that he was clinically sterile. One night I had an affair with a black man (my husband and I are white) and became pregnant. Woe is me, I thought. I worried and thought and worried some more and was about ready to go have an abortion. That's when I had the dream. In the dream, there was a cliff by the ocean. It was rather a windy, misty place. Standing by the edge of the cliff was a young woman, in her early twenties, with her back to me. She turned around to face me and I knew it was my daughter. I don't know how I knew, I just knew it. I don't remember a voice telling me so, but I do remember the sense of knowing."

After that dream, Patti told her husband everything. "Right up to the minute Ronnie was born he wasn't sure that it was his child. But I knew. She'll be fifteen soon and she looks exactly like the young woman in my dream-vision. It was her eyes that I remember the most. They were gray surrounding brown, just like my daughter's eyes are now becoming.

"That vision had such an impact on me I can still see it in my mind's eye."

The child resembles her father, Patti's husband. Patti is still happily married, and she and her husband have another daughter and a son. So much for being sterile.

Michael, a father in British Columbia reports, "My wife dreamed of rocking a young boy with blond hair two weeks after learning she was pregnant. She had had a similar dream two years prior to her pregnancy.

In July 1992, she gave birth to a seven pound eight ounce boy with blond hair.

"During her second pregnancy, she dreamed of a young girl with dark hair. This described our second child."

For another example, Margaret, an artist and mother in Virginia, reports a probable announcing dream with the common motif of the child appearing older. "During my last pregnancy, whenever I dreamed about the baby it was a boy," Margaret recalls. "He was larger and more mature than a newborn would be. This was quite different from the baby I thought I was carrying—a petite girl. When my son Andrew was born he was indeed a boy and much larger than my last son."

Another expectant mother, Della, had a dream in which her child was older. "While pregnant with my son," Della reports, "in my dream I saw him looking like he did at age seven. I described the child to my husband, even down to the hairstyle and glasses he wore in the dream.

"As a child, he didn't need glasses until he was seven."

NAMING DREAMS

Naming dreams, a variation of the announcing dream, share a similar theme while revealing information about the unborn child. In the dream, the baby seems to announce his or her name to the mother, father, or other family member.

During naming dreams, the baby often presents itself as a toddler or growing child, rather than an unborn or newborn. For example, Linda, a first-time mother living in Boston, experienced a probable naming dream. She recalls, "My husband Greg and I and our family had a feeling I was carrying a boy. A few days before birth, however, I had a dream about my baby, who in the dream was approximately a year old. The baby's name was Hannah, and I had a very clear visual picture of her.

"I did give birth to a girl and named her Hannah. At one year of age she was exactly as the child in my dream."

Of course, there is no way for the mother to be sure the child really looks just as he or she did in the dream. The elements of dreams are quickly forgotten, particularly years later. The dreamer may therefore unconsciously distort the image of the child in the dream so the dream child looks like the real person. However, such details as blond hair and blue eyes in the dream of a Mediterranean woman with dark hair are unlikely to be forgotten.

In another episode, Paul, a father of two girls and a university computer teacher in the Vancouver area, had a probable naming dream that changed his and his wife Gail's preconceptions about their unborn child.

There was something unique about the dream. It was accompanied by what he calls "an absolute heartfelt certainty that the dream was real." He has had precognitive dreams in the past with the same sense of certainty.

"Both Gail and I felt that our second child would be a boy," recalls Paul. "After the dream, however, I *knew* the girl I had met in my dream was coming. This knowing was an emotional rather than intellectual knowledge. I was just sure—I knew, though I must confess to last-minute doubts in the delivery room.

"On Tuesday, February 8, 1989, my [first] daughter, Anne (who was three years old at the time of my dream), and I go looking for another child to include in our family," Paul recalls of his dream. "We find a large family living in a shack. A small (one-year-old) girl is naked and has clearly not been taken care of properly. Her bottom is not wiped clean.

"She comes to me and I pick her up and hug her. I call her my little penguin, and I know her name is Penelope. Her parents don't care if she comes with me. She is very happy to find a family who will love her and care for her. She seems a quite placid individual.

"When I picked up Penelope, she hugged me with tremendous strength, really locking on to me.

"My daughter was born on August 23 (my birthday), 1989. My wife wouldn't agree to the name Penelope, so we named her Valerie. Valerie hugs exactly the same as the child in the dream. Anne doesn't.

"I don't remember her face clearly, but I remember her personality. She was a generally calm and humorous child in her first few years. We've both remarked that she behaves like someone who has been here before. We neither believe nor disbelieve in reincarnation."

The following seems to be a waking version of a naming dream the father experienced while meditating. Randy reports: "My partner, Amber, and I found out about our pregnancy in late October of last year. The night before she was to have a pregnancy test, I perceived with my eyes closed a small point of light coming from her uterine region. I realized that she was indeed pregnant. The next day we knew for sure. A month or two later we were discussing potential names for the new arrival and I decided to ask the baby who he or she was. The response I received was that his name was Alexander. By the time he was born (May 23, 1993), Amber was firmly convinced she was carrying a girl. I disagreed. Later she give birth to a healthy boy."

PRODROMAL DREAMS

Prodromal dreams reveal facts about current conditions. These intuitive dreams are usually the result of the expectant mother's characteristic heightened awareness of subtle signals from her body rather than extrasensory perception.

Marryn had a never-to-be-forgotten nightmare. In this graphic dream of terror she recalls: "I was in a meat factory and was thrown into a meat grinder. I woke up sweating and screaming. I knew then that the baby wasn't going to be born."

Everyone has nightmares from time to time, especially during pregnancy when so many concerns and worries surface. But there was something different about this dream. During the dream, and immediately after waking, Marryn knew it was directly connected to her child's well-being. She associated the horrible images in this dream with films she had seen of aborted babies years before. "After I woke up, I cried for a long time because of the associations that I had with the abortion films I had seen in high school."

A few days later, Marryn suffered a miscarriage.

Brenda, another expectant mother, had the following apparently prodromal vision while meditating. "A week or so after I conceived—not thinking I was pregnant because I had used contraception during my previous sexual encounters—I had a vision while meditating. I first saw a house. It then turned into a baby. It felt very nice so I really started to focus on it thinking it must be some important symbol. The experience soon changed and I suddenly felt like I was giving birth. It felt really beautiful and I remember thinking how wonderful it would be to actually have a child one of these days. A few weeks later I got the result of a pregnancy test back and to my surprise was actually pregnant." This lovely vision was probably inspired by subtle changes already occurring in Brenda's body.

PRECOGNITIVE DREAMS

Precognitive dreams, among the most perplexing and inexplicable of all intuitive phenomena, reveal facts about future events. A problem with these mysterious dreams is that one usually has no way of knowing whether or not the dream is true precognition until after the fact.

Donna-Lynne, a freelance clerical worker, had a remarkable precognitive dream of her uncle about two weeks before her daughter Stephanie was born. Donna-Lynne's first two pregnancies had ended in miscarriages and she had experienced a threatened miscarriage with Stephanie.

Donna-Lynne recalls: "Uncle Carl was constantly reassuring and encouraging me. It wasn't that he was saying anything different than what the doctors were telling me, rather that he seemed able to impart a confidence I could believe.

"In the dream, Uncle Carl was standing in a meadow lush with vegetation. There was a hill in the background. He seemed to be younger in the dream than he was in real life.

"He spoke to me, telling me that I was going to be okay and the baby would be fine. He said he would like to be there after the birth but wouldn't be able to, except in spirit. Then he turned and walked toward the hill. When he reached the top of the hill, he turned back toward me and waved. Then he turned again and walked over the hill, which was backlit very brightly, as if the sun were just about to rise there.

"Stephanie was born on October 1. There were complications during the delivery. I began to hemorrhage so had to remain in the hospital a few days. We left the hospital on October 4. Uncle Carl died that night."

Is this the result of telepathic communication with her uncle? Or is it genuine precognition? It's impossible to say. However, Donna-Lynne experienced additional dreams earlier in pregnancy that strongly suggest precognitive awareness.

She dreamed a number of dreams, each involving a major fire. "I had a clock radio that was set to wake me at 7:00 A.M. for work," she recalls. "I vividly remember hearing a broadcast about a three-alarm fire located less than a block from where I was then working. On account of this, I gave myself extra travel time to avoid being late for work.

"When I arrived at work, however, there were no indications of a fire—no smoke, no trucks, no police, no detours. I told several of the other secretaries about the broadcast and asked if they had heard the news. All responded in the negative.

"Later that afternoon, our building was evacuated and the employees sent home after a fire broke out in a building close to ours. The police must have heard me and the other secretaries talking about it on the sidewalk. The following day a policeman and a fire chief questioned me. No official action was taken."

For no apparent reason, Donna-Lynne heard the news of two additional fires before they occurred. Why did Donna-Lynne's unconscious mind select fire reports as a target for her paranormal experiences? Without knowing her personal history, there is really no way of telling. However, in general, paranormal experiences, like ordinary dreams, seem to involve themes of particular interest to the person having the experience.

Geraldine, a saleswoman in San Diego and mother of two, had probable precognitive dreams just prior to conceiving both her children.

"When we wanted a second child," Geraldine reports, "I'd take my temperature and record it on a graph to determine the optimal time for conception and I realized I was going to be away at a convention during that time.

"That night I dreamed I was in a beautiful motel lobby with a brick floor that seemed to have been laminated. I was telling my friend, who accompanied me on the trip, that I was pregnant."

When Geraldine later visited the motel, she saw the same lobby she had seen in the dream. "When I got inside the motel where we were to be staying," recalls Geraldine, "the floor was indeed brick with a thick coat of some kind of shiny stuff on top. At the time, I thought: 'How am I to become pregnant when my husband's home and I'm here? I discounted it as a ridiculous dream.

"The following week I found out I was indeed pregnant."

At first glance, this dream looks like a prodromal rather than precognitive dream. Geraldine was probably pregnant before the dream and unconsciously sensed subtle physical changes.

But that doesn't explain seeing the motel lobby before she arrived. Feeling subtle changes in one's body can be explained without recourse to the paranormal. Seeing a motel lobby miles away one has never visited cannot.

Nor can Geraldine's dream about her second pregnancy.

"I dreamed that I became pregnant in a basement apartment—a place I had never seen. I remember something in the dream about suns on the floor and pennies scattered around somewhere."

A few days later, while apartment hunting, she saw the basement apartment of her dream. "The carpet had a sunburst pattern!" reports Geraldine. "I knew then this was the home where I would become pregnant with my second child."

But what about the pennies? Geraldine didn't see any pennies—until the tenant who then lived in the apartment opened the closet door. The tenant apologized. She had recently dropped a bank. "Pennies were scattered everywhere," recalls Geraldine.

Sadly, most memorable precognitive dreams foreshadow tragedy. For example, when Sheryl, a nurse, was approximately eight weeks pregnant with her third child, Robert, she had a terrible nightmare that her entire family had been killed. The dream was different from most nightmares.

"I usually don't remember my nightmares," Sheryl recalls, "but this was different. It felt like I had been hit by lightning in slow motion. I felt it from my head to the tips of my fingers and the tips of my toes. It was a bone-chilling feeling. I've never forgotten that dream.

"From the time I had that dream until after the birth, I had an intuitive feeling that a death would occur. And I knew it would be the baby. I don't know why I felt that way. It was just a weird intuitive-type feeling."

That terrible dream left an indelible mark on Sheryl.

"While working at the hospital during the pregnancy," she recalls, "I frequently had thoughts like 'How will it feel to come back to work after a maternity leave, and have nothing to show off?' 'How will I explain this to the kids?' 'Why do I know this isn't just one of those common motherly worries?' I remember trying to convince myself that I was simply being morbid, but not believing this.

"Not at all."

Within a few weeks of Robert's birth, Sheryl's family discovered the baby had inexplicably died in his crib, a victim of the dreaded sudden infant death syndrome (SIDS).

"Two weeks prior to his two-month birthday, Sheryl recalls, "I remember begging Robert to hang on for just two more weeks and he would be all right. Somehow I knew that if he made it to that two-month mark, he would be fine. He died at the age of seven weeks.

"When I found Robert in his bassinet, the same feeling I had in the dream washed over me. That very same feeling! Along with this came a horrible feeling of déjà vu—the weirdest and most horrible physical feeling I have ever experienced."

When the outcome of a precognitive dream occurs, it is often accompanied by a feeling of déjà vu—a sense of having lived through or experienced the event before. Accompanied or closely related to the déjà vu feeling is often a sense of the uncanny, a feeling most people have difficulty describing.

Nevertheless, it bears repeating: most pregnancy nightmares are just that—nightmares without any hidden intuitive meaning and no cause for alarm.

During her fourth pregnancy, Sheryl had many nightmares. However, about this pregnancy, she recalls, "I have nothing but feelings of warmth and calm coming from this baby. I have the feeling that he is going to be the best baby I've had—[with] the calmest, quietest disposition."

Sheryl recently gave birth to a healthy boy.

SHARED DREAMS

Psychologists Montague Ullmann and Stanley Krippner of Maimonides Medical Center in New York embarked on what probably remains history's most fascinating dream research project.

The experiment consisted of sending telepathic images to persons in REM sleep. While one person slept, another in a separate room concentrated on a sending a message with vivid, emotional human interest value. The investigators used every imaginable precaution to insure against falsification or possible "leakage" of material.

The uncanny occurred. The dreamer consistently weaved details into his or her dream that had been selected at random and sent "telepathically."[24] The researchers concluded that the vast majority experienced dream telepathy in this controlled setting. Moreover, telepathy occurred regardless of profession, lifestyle, waking intuitive ability, or previous ESP experience.

Experts in the field of dream research believe the right brain hemisphere is more active during sleep. Since—according to current parapsychological theory—the right hemisphere is also the domain of extrasensory perception, this may be the reason why dream telepathy is so effective.

At any rate, shared dreaming is probably far more common than most people realize. The phenomenon occurs frequently during pregnancy.

Mother and child may even share dream patterns, sleeping in synchrony. For example, Swiss pediatrician Dr. Peter Stirnimann studied the sleeping patterns of the unborn child. He discovered that the unborn adjusted to the mother's sleeping patterns and slept when she slept.

Monitoring a group of pregnant women, he found that those who were early morning risers and those who were late risers had babies with similar sleep patterns after birth. The sleep of the newborn is often a continuation of the sleep patterns developed in utero. One expectant mother who woke every night and from 2:00 to 4:00 A.M. to study found that, after giving birth, her baby would wake at 2:00 A.M. and go back to sleep again at 4:00 A.M..[25] In some instances, this may be an episode of telepathy between mother and child. For instance, Laura, a Manhattan businesswoman, found that during the first few months of life her daughter Isabel woke shortly after Laura woke and thought of her. "All I had to do," Laura recalls, "was think of her to make her wake up. If I woke in the middle of the night and thought about her, within a few seconds she would start stirring and making sounds in her nursery, wanting to be fed. It seemed that she was picking up on my thoughts in her sleep."

In her extensive research about the dream life of expectant parents, Dr. Maybruck has observed that fathers-to-be frequently have telepathic dreams, sharing dreams images and scenarios with their mates."[26]

INTUITIVE DREAM OR NOT?

Intuitive dreams may be the expectant mother's way of transcending her ego boundaries and linking with nature, the universe. But how can you tell the difference between an intuitive dream and an ordinary dream? In essence, the characteristics of precognitive and other paranormal dreams are vividness, the conviction that the dream is real, and, often, a sense of the uncanny. However, no single set of guidelines works for every person, except in the event of shared dreams when the symbols can be later verified for accuracy. Like all forms of intuition, people often find it difficult to convey the experience. Moreover, the hallmarks of intuition vary from one person to another.

Margaret, who has had accurate dreams about her own unborn child, reports: "What distinguishes these dreams from ordinary dreams is the feeling that they are real—that they are not just ordinary dreams and there is always something just a little surreal about them."

It is wise to keep a journal of dreams you think may be intuitive, particularly if the dream concerns your unborn child. Frequently, you don't know if the dream was truly an intuition until after the baby is born.

A woman who has frequent paranormal dreams reports on the difference between her precognitive and ordinary nightmares: "Nightmares are usually associated with terror or horror. My dreams that have announced something didn't have this feeling. They were more indifferent, like newscasts.

"I once had a dream that I saw headlines in several different newspapers announcing a classmate had died. I found out the next night that he had indeed been admitted to the hospital with complications from a recent surgery of which I had no previous knowledge. Later, when he returned to school, he said he had been declared clinically dead during that emergency!"

Another primary difference between intuitive and ordinary dreaming is that the ordinary dream comes from the contents of one's own unconscious mind and one's experience. *The intuitive dream reveals information beyond immediate experience.*

TAPPING THE POWER OF SHARED DREAMS

You can use the dreams you and your partner share to better adjust to pregnancy's life-transforming changes.

Here are some suggestions:

- Compare dream images and scenarios with your mate. See how many, if any, are actually similar and seem to be more than just coincidence.

- Keep a journal and write down those that turn out to be genuine intuitions.

- When one of you is waking and the other sleeping, you may even want to try sending a vivid emotionally meaningful image (keep the image positive!). Either create the image in your imagination, use an image with emotional meaning to both of you, or select it from a magazine, book, artwork, or the like.

As useful as intuitive dreams can sometimes be, it is usually wise to ignore nightmares and foreboding, as these can cause unnecessary worry. Pregnancy is a life crisis. You, your partner, and the family are all undergoing a revolution. The last thing you need is additional worry about dreams that are probably just dreams.

If, however, you have a specific concern that a dream may be giving you a warning, consult your physician or midwife. If your health provider passes this off as nonsense, by all means seek another health care provider. Generally speaking, midwives are more experienced handling the emotional and intuitive elements of pregnancy than are general practitioners or obstetricians.

Following are common distinguishing features of intuitive dreams. Bear in mind, however, that these characteristics do not apply to all intuitive dreams. Nor does having one or more of these characteristics mean you have had an extrasensory experience. They are *only guidelines*.

Intuitive dreams

- are frequently more vivid than other dreams
- are sometimes accompanied by a distinct feeling that this is something you should pay attention to
- are sometimes accompanied by a sense of the uncanny or a feeling that there is something dramatically unusual about the dream
- are often specific—rather than dreaming there is something wrong with her child, the mother may dream the child is experiencing a specific complication such as being choked by the umbilical cord

RECALLING DREAMS

Dream exercises can help you unveil a source of anxiety, uncover the hidden meaning of a dream symbol, create the conditions for a healing dream, dream about a topic of your choice, and even tap your intuition to request specific information in a dream.[27] Heeding probable intuitive dreams may even help expectant parents resolve potential complications.

For example, an expectant mother who dreams there is something wrong with her baby may seek further testing and medical help, which could very well save the life of her child. Dreams can give you insight into your feelings, even enlist the aid of your unconscious mind in enjoying a healthier pregnancy, making better birth plans, and preparing for your new lives as mother and father.

If you'd like to try tapping intuition in dreams, here are some suggestions gleaned from experts in the field of dreams:

- Pay greater attention to your dreams. Many people claim that they don't dream. More likely, however, they simply don't remember their dreams.
- Try keeping a dream record to recall dreams more vividly.
- Write down your dreams shortly upon awakening. You may even want to keep pencil and paper by your bed and write down your images.

- To enhance dream recall, lie in bed a few minutes with eyes closed, thinking about your dream images to fix them in mind, then write them down.
- Try to awaken naturally, if at all possible. Little can chase a dream away more effectively than a clanging alarm clock you want to throw out the window.
- Try a relaxation exercise or guided imagery exercise before going to sleep.
- As you drift off to sleep, mentally repeat a strong positive statement such as "I will remember my dream when I wake up," a few times silently to yourself. Then drift off to sleep naturally.

DREAM MAKING

In ancient Greece, people made pilgrimages to the temples of Aesculapius, the god of healing. After ritually cleansing their bodies, they slept in a sacred place where they had dreams giving them instructions for healing.[28]

You can do the same thing today in your own home. And during pregnancy, when the right-hemisphere is more active and you are in closer touch with your unconscious mind, you may find the methods of creating dreams in this chapter quite effective.

INCUBATING A DREAM

- Tell yourself what you would like to dream about as you are drifting off to sleep.
- If you wish, begin with a relaxation method just before going to sleep. Try a relaxation or guided imagery exercise.
- While doing the exercise, give yourself an affirmation such as "I will dream about . . ." (and name the topic). Repeat the affirmation several times before falling asleep.
- Pose a question to your inner mind as you fall asleep. Formulate the question as clearly as you are able. Ask your inner mind for a solution, then drift off to sleep.

Dream incubation is the process of deliberately creating a dream. Some people successfully decide to have a dream about a specific subject or are able to use dreams to answer specific problems. They "incubate" or "hatch" the dream while falling asleep.

Dream incubation can help resolve recurrent nightmares. For example, Maybruck recalls a dramatic tale of the healing power of an incubated dream in her book *Pregnancy and Dreams*. Martha, a twenty-six-year-old secretary, had a terrifying dream of being at home with another woman and a stranger was lurking outside. "This crazy weird-looking stranger told my mother he was going to hurt me somehow," Martha recalls. She decided to follow the steps described above to create her own dream and resolve the nightmare. In response, she had a symbolic and quite moving dream.

"This time," Martha says of the dream, "I see that the woman is my mother." Her mother tells Martha to invite the threatening stranger inside. Martha opens the door. "Who are you? What do you want from me?" she demands of the stranger. The stranger grows bigger and bigger until finally he takes on gigantic proportions. Then the giant smiles and tells Martha, "I am your birth power. If you let me stay here in the house, I'll help you bring the baby outside. But if you fight me, then I'll have to hurt you!" And just before Martha wakes, her mother says in the dream: "You see, I told you we had to let him inside."

The message Martha received from her dream applies to all women, all parents. As the mother surrenders to the power of birth—a giant by any standard—it becomes our ally rather than our adversary.

The *lucid dream* is another uncommon form of dream, during which the dreamer is actually conscious yet continues to dream. This is quite different from dreaming you are awake. During the lucid dream, the dreamer really is conscious and alert. With lucid dreams, some people are able to control their dream images. As with other talents, some people can accomplish lucid dreaming with little effort while others are not able to achieve this ability. Don't be concerned if you can't create a lucid dream even after following the steps outlined below. This is perfectly normal.

Dr. Stephen LaBerge, a dream expert, has designed an easy-to-follow method to develop lucid dreaming. The following steps are adapted from his method[29] and dream expert Patricia Maybruck's suggestions.[30]

LUCID DREAMING

- When you wake from a dream, remain calm with your eyes closed as you mentally recall the dream.
- Then, repeatedly give yourself an affirmation such as "In my next dream, I want to know what I am dreaming."
- Next, recall the dream again and imagine you are reexperiencing the dream (even though you are still awake).
- Finally, drift back to sleep, while you repeatedly recall the images of the recent dream, imagining that you are aware that you are dreaming.

INTUITIVE DREAM-MAKING

To enhance your chance of experiencing an intuitive dream, take the same steps as described in *"Incubating a Dream,"* then ask yourself a specific question about your pregnancy, your baby, or your birth plans. Or tell yourself something even more specific like "I will have a dream about . . . ," then name a specific situation or event. Bear in mind that intuitive dreams can embody either intuition that is explicable in terms of ordinary psychology and science or ESP.

If you receive an insight from this method, it may be very fleeting. People who use this method frequently recommend either keeping a pencil and paper by the bed to write down the insight immediately upon waking or making a deliberate attempt to commit the insight to memory.

You can use an incubated dream to tap your intuition. For example, Sandra, a first-time mother in Calgary, wanted to dream about her baby, to actually see her baby in the womb. After several tries, she achieved this lovely intuitive dream:

"I dreamed my abdomen became transparent and I could see our baby floating inside. Immediately I knew I was dreaming because this couldn't happen in real life."

Sandra woke at this point. She repeatedly told herself she wanted the dream to continue as she fell back to sleep. "I dreamed of the baby in my uterus again, only this time I was there, too. Again, I knew I was dreaming—only this time I didn't wake. We were floating or swimming underwater, but I could breathe and talk. It was amazing. The water was pale blue and our baby was glowing pink. The cord was sort of a turquoise color, luminescent. It was breathtaking, so beautiful! Then I said to the baby, 'Turn over, darling, so I can see if you're a boy or girl.' The baby smiled and rolled its little body toward me. It was a boy with long dark hair and huge green eyes."

This exquisite announcing dream, deliberately evoked by the mother, was indeed a journey to the womb. Donna later gave birth to a green-eyed boy with long, dark hair.[31]

Don't be concerned if you can't make dreams occur at will. This method doesn't work immediately. Most people have to make several attempts before successfully incubating a dream. Some never master this technique. This is perfectly normal.

CHAPTER 8

NESTING

A glimpse at pregnancy's dream life suggests that the growing abdomen is not all that expands during the months of gestation. As nauseous and fatigued as she may sometimes feel, the pregnant woman radiates a vitality and almost magnetic aura that touches all around her. Being "with child" confers special status on her. Everyone's attention turns to her. Her family shows concern. Friends offer help. People make comments. Even strangers smile, begin conversations, and express congratulations as if she carries with her a magic potion causing every eye to turn her way. The vitality of creating new life seems somehow to "spill over" from the expectant mother and sometimes affects her family and friends. It appears almost as if pregnancy has an undiscovered component that radiates from the mother and broadcasts a message to those around her. Relatives and friends often sense pregnancy has occurred.

Even when the expectant mother is on the other side of the world.

This is what occurred when Simone, a new mother in Pittsburgh, Pennsylvania, became pregnant with her third and fourth children. Her cousin Carol Ann, an engineer from Cleveland, Ohio, hadn't seen Simone in seven months.

"I was traveling in Europe at the time," Carol Ann recalls. "While relaxing in my hotel in Geneva, Switzerland, I had an odd feeling like remembering something someone said but couldn't recall who said it. I thought, 'Simone is pregnant.'

"My husband and I were getting ready to go out to dinner when I asked him if someone had told us that she was pregnant. The thought had occurred to me several times before, but that was the first time I spoke up about it."

There was no reason for Carol Ann to suspect her cousin was pregnant. In fact, she had good reason to think the opposite. Simone was a new mother who had given birth only a few months earlier.

"When I returned home," Carol Ann continues, "I called my Dad, who lives near Simone, and asked him if she were pregnant. He said, 'No! She just had a baby!'"

A month later Carol Ann's sister told her that Simone was indeed pregnant again and had been when Carol Ann was touring Europe.

Though intuition occurs throughout pregnancy, as the time of birth draws near, intuitive experiences frequently become more common. The energy of creating new life becomes almost palpable, like the atmosphere before a storm. The mother's intuition heightens. Simultaneously, her almost magnetic aura, seems to embrace her family, friends, sometimes even her health care provider.

THE NESTING INSTINCT

Perhaps the baby announces his or her arrival in a form of intuition so common almost every parent experiences it: *the nesting instinct.*

Our first son, Carl, was born in a hospital where my wife, Jan, had first-rate medical care. The obstetrician who attended the birth, Leo Sorger, is a prominent and highly skilled New England physician. He is also one of those rare physicians fully committed to helping parents give birth the way they choose. The dimly lit room where Carl was born was peaceful, pleasant, and comfortable. The birth was one of the peak experiences of our lives.

Despite our positive in-hospital experience, however, we couldn't dismiss the fact that leaving our comfortable home in the middle of the night to go to a hospital, a place associated with sickness, had been unnecessarily traumatic. Beginning a family is a tremendously emotional time for the new parents—to say nothing of the baby. We felt it should take place at home.

When our second son, Paul, was born, we were living in an apartment in Brookline, Massachusetts. Since our apartment never quite felt like home, we arranged to rent a house on a hill in central Vermont for the birth. There, I "caught" our second son, Paul, as Dr. Thurmond Knight, a now-retired family physician, played Renaissance flute while standing by to help if necessary.

SIGNS OF IMPENDING LABOR

The mother's or father's intuition is often the first and most accurate sign that labor will soon begin. Here are the others:

- Lightening and engagement
- Discharge of the mucous plug, or "bloody show"
- An increase in Braxton-Hicks contractions
- A decrease in fetal movements
- Diarrhea
- Rupture of membranes and loss of water through the vagina (about 15% of mothers)
- A spurt of energy
- The *nesting instinct*

Two weeks before Paul was due to be born, I was sitting with my wife at the dinner table. Suddenly, I felt an overwhelming urge to unpack our birth supplies and get the baby's cradle ready. At first I ignored this feeling, since the baby was not due for another two weeks. Nor had Jan experienced any of the classic signs associated with impending labor.

Most women experience several indications that labor is soon to begin. There was little chance the birth of Paul was imminent, since we had seen no prelabor signs. Except one: the urge to prepare the birthplace and the baby's temporary home—a phenomenon called the *nesting instinct*, typically ascribed to the expectant mother, not the father. The nesting urge grew so strong I finally mentioned it to Jan.

That's when I learned she had been feeling the same urge though she hadn't mentioned it. Fortunately we paid attention to the intuition and got everything ready for the baby. Only a few hours later, Jan unexpectedly went into labor. Paul, our second son, was born the following morning.

The nesting instinct—as we discovered for ourselves—is most definitely one of the signs of impending labor! Toward the end of pregnancy, the mother-to-be, and sometimes the expectant father, frequently have a sudden burst of energy accompanied by a strong urge to prepare a place for the soon-to-be-arriving new family member. Labor almost invariably begins within twenty-four to forty-eight hours.

What causes this phenomenon? Is it hormonally mediated? Does the baby somehow broadcast an announcement that she or he will soon be entering the world? No one really knows. Of all the signs of impending labor, the nesting instinct is the most unaccountable. Every textbook describes it, but no one knows the cause. The nesting instinct lets the parents know labor is on the way often even in the absence of other prelabor signs. Paying heed to this intuition and making last minute preparations for the baby's new home helps both parents to adjust to the transformation childbirth will bring as the physical activity helps the mother prepare for labor.

INTUITIONS OF LABOR

Though the nesting instinct usually bursts on one's consciousness with a flush of energy, other labor intuitions are often far more subtle.

THE NESTING INSTINCT

Heeding the nesting instinct, one of the most common but inexplicable signs of impending labor, benefits the parents in the following ways:

1. It assists the parents to make last minute preparations for the baby's new home.
2. It may prepare the parents psychologically for the new family member.
3. The surge of energy and physical activity that usually accompanies the nesting instinct may help the mother experience a shorter labor.

The expected date of birth, many parents-to-be are surprised to learn, is only an approximation. It is accurate to the day only two to five percent of the time. *More often than not, the baby is born within two weeks before or after the "due date."* However, expectant parents frequently have intuitions *of the precise time labor will begin.*

Evelyn, a Vermont mother of two, had a beautiful vision of a great mother goddess figure while half-sleeping. "While dozing I could feel and see an Earth Mother figure hovering close to me," recalls Evelyn. "She looked very much like the ancient symbols—large, pendulous breasts over an enormous bulging belly ready for birth. I realized my instincts were telling me I would soon be giving birth. I accepted the Earth Mother as my new self-image."

The following morning, Evelyn went into labor.

This labor intuition was likely the result of early labor contractions, sometimes called *prodromal labor*. The contractions were apparently not forceful enough to wake Evelyn and command the attention of her conscious mind. Instead, her unconscious probably gave birth to the intuition that labor was on the way in the form of the beautiful mythic image.

Sometimes the expectant mother or father may intuit labor in advance of its onset, something that is unlikely to be explained in terms of subliminally perceived physical perceptions. For example, toward the end of our own first pregnancy, Jan and I felt our son Carl would be born on the following weekend, even though Jan had no signs of impending labor. We were so sure of the intuition that we canceled our Monday appointment with Jan's obstetrician. Our first son, Carl, was born on Sunday morning at 5:59 A.M.

No one knows what causes labor to begin when it does. One theory holds that hormones passed between mother and baby trigger labor to begin. New Zealand fetologist Sir William Liley says that the initiation of labor is a joint venture between mother and baby.[1]

"Far from being an inert passenger in a pregnant mother," he writes, "the fetus is very much in command of the pregnancy. It is the fetus who guarantees the endocrine success of pregnancy and induces all manner of changes in maternal physiology. . . . It is the fetus who determines the duration of pregnancy. It is the fetus who decides which way he will lie in pregnancy and which way he will present in labor."[2]

Whatever causes labor's beginning, many parents have reported knowing the time their child would be born in advance. Marryn, a graphic designer and fine artist in Seattle, Washington, recalls knowing the precise day her child would be born many weeks before the birth. "I knew for a fact that Colleen was going to be born on the first of May, even though this was three and a half weeks after my due date." This is especially remarkable considering it is uncommon for a child to be born more than two weeks after the expected date of birth. However, Marryn's intuition proved accurate.

"I went into labor at the end of April," Marryn recalls. "After forty-eight hours of hard labor without cervical dilatation, I finally had a cesarean on May first. Colleen was born healthy."

Like many other intuitive experiences during pregnancy, the labor intuition is often unconscious or so subtle that it skims by beneath the surface of our awareness.

Unconscious "slips" during the course of conversation, many health care practitioners have found, may reveal the parents' intuitive knowledge of the date of birth. For example, while making some future plans it is not uncommon for the mother to say, "The baby will be born before Harry's birthday" without realizing she may be expressing an intuitive knowledge of the time of birth.

As one midwife puts it: "There is no biological explanation for this but mothers seem to sense when their baby will be born—even weeks before the due date. A week or so before giving birth, a client will phone to cancel an appointment. Or she will neglect to make a new appointment as if a part of her mind already knows that she will not be able to keep it."

The mother's thoughts may even be able to control the time of labor's onset.

Expectant mothers frequently hold their labor back without realizing it. For example, many maternity care providers have noticed that their clients "wait" to begin labor until the care provider returns from a vacation.

By sending thoughts and images to the yet unborn child, the mother may even be able to influence her labor. As Donald Creevy, M.D., assistant professor of obstetrics at Stanford University in California, puts it: "By relaxing and letting the baby know her wishes and expectations, the mother may be able to influence the time of birth."

CAN INTUITION PREVENT COMPLICATIONS?

In the course of prenatal research, health professionals have discovered that the power of thoughts to influence labor's onset may very well have far-reaching consequences. The mind may actually be able to help prevent pregnancy complications.

Though the precise cause of labor's onset remains an enigma, one theory holds that hormones passed between mother and baby trigger labor to begin. If this is so, *transuterine communication* may sometimes resolve and even prevent a wide range of pregnancy and birth complications from miscarriage to prolonged labor. For example, the exercise "Communicating With Your Unborn Child" (introduced in chapter 6) occasionally has dramatic results prior to and during labor. One woman, thought to have a *postmature* (overdue) labor, was scheduled to receive hormonal induction. Yet, while doing the exercise, she clearly felt, "My baby is not ready to be born." Further testing showed that the due date had been miscalculated and the baby was still not fully developed.

Needless to say, an intuition such as this should be confirmed in the light of common sense and, when possible, with appropriate medical diagnostics before acting on it.

Most conventional health professionals believe complications such as miscarriage and prematurity are primarily physical in cause. And no doubt they often are. Adequate nutrition through pregnancy, avoiding unnecessary health risks such as cigarette smoking, and getting regular prenatal care sum up the conventional practitioner's advice for preventing these conditions. Nevertheless, approximately 7 percent of pregnancies end in premature labor and some of the prematurely born babies die.

Recently retired obstetrician David Cheek, holds what may be the most radical view in the world of obstetrics about these all-too-common complications. In striking contrast to his colleagues, he believes emotional and even parapsychological factors are as important as organic ones in causing childbirth complications, including hemorrhage, miscarriage, toxemia of pregnancy (also called preeclampsia, a condition characterized by high blood pressure, excessive fluid retention, and other problems usually linked with diet), and even mechanical cervical problems such as "incompetent cervix" (the cervix does not remain closed throughout pregnancy)—a major cause of premature labor.[3] All of these complications may be related and sometimes stem from similar emotional stresses.[4]

Obviously genuine physical problems, which are sometimes unavoidable, can precipitate miscarriage or other pregnancy complications. *No mother who experiences a miscarriage, premature labor, or other pregnancy complication should blame her thoughts.* However, by the same token, fears, superstitions, guilt feelings, and resentment can *sometimes* affect uterine function.[5]

Dr. Cheek believes the baby can initiate an early labor in response to the mother's unconscious fear, which she may communicate telepathically. "The expectant mother worries something is wrong," he says. "Her fear may even come out in a dream. If the dream is not brought to consciousness, she may continue the same dream successive nights."

If the baby fears it is not safe to be inside, she or he may initiate labor. External things can frighten the mother. It is the obstetrician's job to address this, but this is usually overlooked. For that matter, obstetricians often do the opposite and create the fear that can initiate labor.[6] If the mother is at high risk of premature labor she may be able to influence the outcome by beaming peaceful thoughts to the preborn child. Of course, this doesn't always work, but it is certainly worth trying, *providing the mother does not see this as a substitute for her physician's or midwife's care.*

"Active and enthusiastic reassurance without hospitalization," Dr. Cheek explains, "would do as well as any other form of treatment for threatened abortion (miscarriage)."[7]

His therapy for miscarriage and premature labor consists of correcting misunderstandings about bleeding in pregnancy, curing emotional problems such as frigidity with hypnosis, discussing the expectant mother's dreams, and remaining positively optimistic in all communication. Of course, the mother attempting this sort of therapy should also accompany this with competent medical care.

When hypnotizing a woman with a threatened miscarriage, Dr. Cheek asks if she feels she could be holding any emotional cause for the bleeding or premature labor. Sometimes repeated sessions are necessary to elicit results.

Once she has explored her inner feelings, Dr. Cheek asks, "Do you think you will have stopped bleeding by the time we finish this conversation?" The client answers by finger motions. If her answer is no, Dr. Cheek continues working with her until she can see herself going forward in her mind's eye to the time labor contractions or bleeding has stopped. It would be easy to write this off as so much wishful thinking if it weren't for one fact: Dr. Cheek's method works.

"After I learned to address the unconscious fears of expectant mothers," says Dr. Cheek, "I no longer had premature babies born in my practice. My percentage of prematurity dropped from 6.6 percent to

2.6 percent." All of the premature babies were over four pounds, two ounces[8] and all survived.

Not everyone achieves the same results as Dr. Cheek. Part of this physician's success may result from his attitude and the positive feelings he conveys to clients. He embraces a style of practice sadly infrequent in modern medical science. He approaches clients as spirit, emotions, mind, and body, not just as a physical collection of symptoms. He advises giving "very strong tacit suggestions that the doctor knows the trouble will stop when the origin has been found. This is in contrast to the usual impression given by doctors."[9]

For decades, other health professionals have observed a connection between the emotions and pregnancy complications.[10] California psychotherapist Gayle Peterson observes, "Women who have had abortions and carry guilt from these experiences tend to be at greater risk for both prematurity and miscarriage. It is not the abortion itself that contributes to this tendency but rather the woman's unresolved feelings that render her vulnerable."[11]

For example, Leanna, a thirty-eight-year-old pregnant second-time mother, had previously aborted a Down's syndrome baby (Down's syndrome is a congenital disorder resulting in physical and mental abnormalities). During her second pregnancy, she began experiencing insomnia and nausea—not uncommon conditions. However, when she tried to picture the baby in the womb during a therapy session with Dr. Peterson, she saw only her first aborted Down's child. Like many expectant mothers in her situation, Leanna was preoccupied with the trauma of the prior abortion.

Through therapy, Dr. Peterson helped Leanna resolve her feelings. The mother-to-be experienced a dramatic change. She was soon able to visualize her baby growing in the womb. This is a sign of the development of parental-infant attachment, or "bonding." Her symptoms disappeared.[12]

Dr. Peterson has also found transuterine communication an effective method of preventing prematurity and miscarriage. Sarah, a first-time mother, went into premature labor at thirty weeks. Dr. Peterson recommended that Sara do an exercise to get in touch with her unborn child.

"In her first session," Peterson recalls, "Sarah cried as we went inside the womb to look at her baby. She felt she did not deserve the baby, that she would not be a good enough mother, and would be unable to take care of her child."

Therapy for Sarah included developing confidence in her capacity as mother and using guided imagery tapes with a message about carrying her pregnancy to term. Her premature labor stopped, and she was able to carry her pregnancy to term.[13]

All of this suggests that the mind and body may be inextricably linked throughout the childbearing experience.

CHAPTER 9

The Metamorphosis of Childbirth

What happens in the mother's body during childbirth appears to be a half-told tale. We can no more reduce the experience of labor to a description of how the cervix dilates and how the baby descends in the birth canal than we can capture love in a test tube or explain satisfying lovemaking in terms of swelling and release in the genital organs.

The laboring woman is a primal elemental being. Vulnerable and emotionally sensitive as she is, she radiates a primal strength, a power, and a beauty that is incomparable to anything else. She seems to be cooperating with a power greater than herself—the life-creating force. The incredible processes that began on the day of conception reach their climax on the day of the archetypal passage rite: birth. When it is time for the baby to leave its warm secure inner universe to greet mom and dad's waiting arms, nature's greatest miracle, the metamorphosis of body and mind that began during pregnancy, reaches its summit.

THE LABORING MIND RESPONSE: KEY TO HEIGHTENED INTUITION

While the dimple-sized cervical opening widens to a gateway for the baby to pass from womb to world, the laboring woman experiences a series of dramatic emotional and behavioral changes that childbirth educators teach as *the laboring mind response.* I developed this concept to help both parents and health professionals better understand what goes on in the mother's mind and emotions as labor progresses.

The laboring mind response consists of seven characteristics, many of which parapsychologists have associated with heightened intuition.

Some of these psychophysiological changes began during pregnancy and become intensified during labor.

First is greater right-brain-hemisphere orientation. As labor progresses, the focus of the laboring woman's energy seems to shift from the logic-oriented, rational left hemisphere of the brain to the intuition-oriented right hemisphere.

A second change the laboring woman undergoes is an altered state of consciousness. She experiences a profound psychological transformation. At labor's onset, she may be anxious, elated, relieved, excited, talkative, and so forth. Yet she is usually able to continue her everyday life. Once labor is under way, however, and contractions continue to dilate the cervix, she seems to enter her own world. Her concentration narrows and she becomes more introspective, or inner focused. Her contractions and the people in her immediate environment become her world.

THE LABORING MIND RESPONSE

During labor, most women experience seven characteristics that, taken together, spell a profound psychological change.

1. Greater right-brain-hemisphere orientation*
2. An altered state of mind in which the mother becomes less rational and more instinctive*
3. Altered perceptions of space and time
4. Heightened emotional sensitivity*
5. Lowered inhibitions
6. Distinctly sexual behavior*
7. Increased openness to suggestion*

*All are qualities that parapsychologists have associated with heightened intuition.

As she experiences this profound psychological transmutation, she becomes less rational, more instinctive, and more intuitive. Providing that nothing, such as the sudden intrusion of strangers, interferes with the delicate balance of the laboring mind response, the mother-to-be's intuition tends to take over. She will follow her instincts and almost invariably choose the best possible birth position to labor for her and her baby—a position that varies from woman to woman, depending on a variety of conditions.

As California midwife Elizabeth Davis observes, "Once labor is well under way, many marvel to find themselves moving, breathing, and taking positions with total spontaneity. This is beautiful to witness, the laboring woman completely vulnerable and yet fully in charge of her experience."[1]

Which isn't surprising. Since her body is able to create the ideal conditions for the growth of a child from a single seed, one would think she would know intuitively how to give birth in the best possible way for that child, what position to assume, how to move, and how to breathe in harmony with her labor contractions.

As labor progresses, and though labor usually becomes more painful, women sometimes become so intuitive that they are often able to sense the thoughts and feelings of others in their birthing environment without even realizing it. This is probably the reason an insensitive physician or midwife, impatient for labor to progress, can actually cause the mother's labor to slow down just by being present in the room. The mother intuits the unspoken hostility or impatience. Perhaps unconsciously, she senses she is not in a safe, caring environment to give birth. Her labor stops.

Often, there are psychosomatic explanations for occurrences like this. For example, the mother sees the tension on the health care provider's face and becomes tense herself. Her tension in turn can cause a longer, more painful labor.

A third change the laboring mother experiences is altered perceptions of space and time. As labor rolls on, space and time seem to become progressively distorted. For example, it is not uncommon for the laboring woman to think her contractions are lasting longer than they actually are.

She becomes so wholly caught up with the forces that are bringing her child into the world that, odd as it may appear to the onlooker, she may even lose sight of the fact that she is going to have a baby. It is as if, in her profoundly altered mind, she forgets the purpose of labor. This state of altered space-time perception—a state of being frequently accompanying intuition—is very similar to experiences people report during deep meditation.

Fourth is heightened emotional sensitivity. Childbirth is one of the most passionate events in a woman's life. Few things compare to seeing a new life enter the world, wet and wriggling. Little compares to that tremendous greeting when parents and child first meet. But there is more to labor's passion than the end result in the miracle of birth. Throughout labor, the mother becomes highly emotional, vulnerable, and sensitive, as if she were reaching a peak of all the mental and emotional changes she experiences during pregnancy. She is utterly dependent on her birth partner and those around her. And her emotions influence her labor profoundly, dramatically, and directly.

Most contemporary people are aware that mind and body are interwoven. Thoughts and feelings affect all physical processes from digestion to blood pressure. However, the relationship of body, mind, emotions, and spirit seems to be nowhere more obvious than during labor when mind and body are inextricably linked.

Childbirth is a deeply moving event. Neither all the word's knowledge about uterine musculature and the complexities of fetal circulation nor all the latest equipment can replace meeting the mother's emotional needs and encouraging her intuition to take over.

The fifth change is lowered inhibitions. As labor progresses toward the end of first stage, women tend to lose their social inhibitions. When she is in an environment conducive to a spontaneous reaction to labor, it is not uncommon to see a laboring woman remove all of her clothing and remain unconcerned about who may see her unclothed body or hear the sensual sounds she makes.

Accepting her uninhibited and intuitive behavior as normal encourages the mother to surrender more easily to labor. Interrupting her, on the other hand, can actually cause her to have a longer, more difficult labor. For instance, in a not uncommon scenario, a father, helping his mate through labor, misinterprets the characteristic laboring sounds as cries of pain and attempts to calm the mother. "Don't do that, honey," the father suggests. He recalls the patterned breathing taught in childbirth classes. "Breathe with me instead!" Then he demonstrates how to pant like a dog on a hot summer day. This well-meant advice can actually interfere with the delicate state of mind labor evokes and cause the mother to become disoriented, perhaps even fight labor rather than surrender to it.

Six, strange as it may first seem, is distinctly sexual behavior. Though few women feel even remotely similar sensations during labor as during lovemaking, there are striking similarities between the two processes. This does not mean labor is a sexual experience or pleasurable. In fact, most women find labor very painful. Yet, in listening to the sounds of a woman during a natural, spontaneous reaction to labor, you may be startled by what you hear. You may even wonder if you are hearing the sounds that caused the pregnancy rather than the sounds of childbirth even though the mother may be experiencing great pain.

You may hear her softly moaning, groaning, and sighing like a woman nearing sexual climax.

Scores of health professionals have commented on it. "The first time I heard a woman giving birth naturally in a childbearing center," says Andrea, a maternity nurse in Michigan, "I was stunned! I felt like I were intruding on someone making love!"

Inexperienced childbirth professionals often misinterpret these sounds as signs of pain. Though vocalizing sometimes indicates a reaction to labor pain, groaning, sighing, and moaning are a normal reaction to labor, often indicating the laboring mother is in an ideal state of mind to give birth most efficiently.

The sexuality of labor deserves special attention because both lovemaking and labor are associated with spontaneous ESP and transpersonal awareness ("peak experiences").

Medical researcher Niles Newton, Ph.D, calls attention to no less than fifteen analogies between the processes that create life and the process that brings life into the world.[2] A brief look at some of these may give us an entirely different orientation on human birth. The most obvious, of course, is that both lovemaking and labor take place in the sexual organs.

During both the early stages of sexual excitement and labor, a woman's breathing becomes faster and deeper. As she approaches orgasm or birth, whichever the case, her breathing may sometimes be interrupted by a catch, a gasp, a sense of holding back before the climax.

As sexual climax approaches and toward the end of labor, a woman's face often wears a tortured yet ecstatic expression[3]—with mouth open, eyes glassy, muscles tense. During both sexual excitement and toward labor's climax in birth, the abdominal muscles and upper uterine segment contract rhythmically, though the contractions are far more noticeable during labor. Sexual excitement and labor cause cervical secretion to loosen the mucus plug ordinarily blocking the opening of the cervix. During lovemaking, cervical secretions loosen to allow the sperm to enter and begin the long upward journey to greet the egg. Throughout pregnancy the mucus plug keeps the gateway sealed to prevent infection. The release of the mucus plug toward the end of pregnancy is one of the first signs that the baby will soon make its journey to mother's waiting arms. The secretion continues to flow through labor.

The physical analogies between lovemaking and labor are only a part of the story. Emotionally, psychologically, and even transpersonally, the two processes share an affinity. During the initial phases of both lovemaking and labor, environmental disturbances can inhibit, if not entirely ruin, the experience. In fact the environment has such a profound impact on labor that it can cause contractions to halt just as surely as a disturbance can decrease sexual arousal. Unfortunately, this point is often overlooked by obstetrical professionals who wonder why a mother's labor sometimes suddenly stops when she is in a highly clinical setting or slows down when strangers enter the room.

LABOR AND LOVEMAKING: UNEXPECTED SIMILARITIES

Striking similarities between labor and lovemaking indicate that both processes may be influenced by similar qualities, such as an emotionally supportive environment.

During both processes, the following changes take place:

- The uterus rhythmically contracts
- The vagina lubricates and opens
- The right-brain hemisphere becomes more active
- A woman becomes intensely emotional, vulnerable
- Emotions and even unspoken thoughts influence the body
- Social inhibitions decrease
- A woman often wears a "tortured-ecstatic" look
- A woman makes similar sounds—moaning, sighing, groaning
- Well-being follows the event
- Spontaneous ESP is common
- Transpersonal experiences are common

Dr. Newton observes both lovemaking and labor "leave the participants particularly vulnerable to outside dangers. Survival, therefore, would be most likely to occur in those individuals and those species that are able to regulate reproductive acts so that they occur in relatively safe surroundings, which elicit calm emotions. It is not surprising that folkways and cultural patterns have long recognized that coitus, parturition, and lactation proceed most smoothly when the surroundings are particularly sheltered or considered to be relatively safe."[4]

During the latter phases of both labor and lovemaking, by contrast, a loss of sensory perception and insensitivity to surroundings occurs. A woman, participating in a process that seems to become greater than the personal self, enters a dreamy state of mind. She may close her eyes and seem to drift into a different world.

After sexual orgasm, there is a sudden return of sensory acuity and alertness. Similarly after giving birth, the mother becomes wide awake, alert, ready to bond with her child, providing medication has not dulled her senses. A feeling of well-being often follows both sexual climax and giving birth. This often includes a flood of joyful emotion and a sense of inner peace.

The seventh characteristic of the laboring mind response is greater openness to suggestion. During the latter phase of labor, the mother seems to enter a quasihypnotic state—strikingly similar to a psychic in trance—during which she is especially open to suggestion.

This greater openness to suggestion may be one reason laboring women find guided imagery—a method of translating positive thoughts into dynamic mental images (discussed ahead)—far more effective in reducing the pain, fear, and length of labor than patterned breathing. For example, a simple exercise such as imagining an opening flower— a metaphor for the dilating cervix—can actually hasten labor's progress. Being familiar with the laboring mind response explains why laboring mothers are especially prone to ESP. It also gives the parents greater insight into the labor experience, enabling them to make plans conducive to a safe, rewarding birth.

TRANSPERSONAL AWARENESS

Like pregnancy, labor also precipitates moments of transpersonal awareness, or "peak experiences." Though labor is undeniably painful for most women, at the same time it is often a richly rewarding experience, one of the high points life has to offer. Both lovemaking and labor induce a peak experience—a sense of something beyond ordinary life. This transpersonal awareness is often described as being connected with and participating in something larger than the self.

One woman describes an unusually vivid lovemaking experience in these powerful words, "I felt at one with my mate, focused on the immediate minute, yet at the same time aware of my essential oneness with all nature and with the universe, larger than life, expanded beyond my personal ego."

Compare this with Seanna's description of labor, an experience that sounds both mystical and sexual. A first-time mother, she had no medication and her experience was unquestionably painful. Yet . . .

"The contractions were like the ocean waves," said Seanna, "wave upon wave, building, peaking, ebbing away, wave upon wave, each wave bringing me further from myself and closer and closer to the heart of creation.

"I felt at one with all nature, with every woman who has ever given birth since the beginning of time."

After the birth of the first of her four boys, Jan, another mother who experienced an intense labor, describes the moments before birth in these terms: "I felt at one with all existence. The contractions were like rivers of energy rushing down a mountain slope, coming through me. I felt like I was taking part in something greater than myself, yet something that was at the same time within me."

Ecstatic descriptions of labor don't refer merely to the joy of greeting the newborn any more than passionate portrayals of lovemaking are inspired by the idea that a child might be conceived during the process. They describe the process itself.

Mystical experiences during labor are as uncommon as they are during lovemaking. Not all women have a sense of being united with the cosmos. In fact, such an experience is the exception rather than the rule. The point is they are more common during labor than at most other times.

RADIANCE OF NEW LIFE

A swirling vortex of energy, the process of labor may affect more than just the mother's body and prepare the baby for its first breath. The laboring woman seems to resonate intuitive experiences in others whether they are in the same room or on the other side of the world. Inexplicable events experienced by other family members are common during birth, as if the miracle of bringing new life into the world were able to reach out and embrace those with whom the mother is emotionally close.

We've discussed how pregnancy sometimes elicits ESP in other family members. The same phenomenon occurs during birth. As birth draws near, other family members, friends, and sometimes health professionals also experience dramatic intuitive episodes. For instance, while Yvette was in labor, a strange thing happened to her sister.

"When I arrived at the hospital the cervix was only dilated two centimeters," Yvette recalls. She had left for the hospital early in labor because she lives in the mountains a considerable distance away. In addition, her family has a history of abrupt births. Her sister and mother met her at the hospital and remained with her and her partner, Barron, during labor. During thirteen hours of labor, Yvette was examined several times but remained at two centimeters.

"After many more hours of labor, I asked to be measured to see if I had reached five centimeters yet. A nurse suggested that I first use the bathroom and then be measured.

"At this time, my sister and mother went across the street to get food for themselves and Barron.

"After I waddled back to my bed from the bathroom, my midwife measured me. Her eyes flew open. 'You're at nine and a half centimeters!' she exclaimed.

"My midwife suggested yielding to the urge to push I was feeling. On the third push I gave birth to my son.

"Meanwhile, as my sister was crossing the street on her way to the restaurant, she knew something was happening. It wasn't a fear, but a sense of certainty my baby was going to be born immediately. She wanted to return to the hospital. She tried to hurry Mom along, but Mom was convinced that my sister was mistaken. After all, the cervix hadn't been dilating for hours.

"They returned just in time to hear my son's first cry."

Such episodes—baffling as they may be—are not uncommon. For example, Andy, a teacher in Minnesota, recalls two times when his wife, Joan, who had never been pregnant herself, sensed when close friends had given birth.

Andy recalls, "On two separate occasions Joan woke up in the morning having dreamed she was giving birth. We later learned that, in both cases, women close to us had given birth on that same day. We hadn't been in contact with one of the women for about a week. In both cases, however, we did know the women were pregnant and we had an idea when they were due."

It is difficult to tell whether this is intuition or just coincidence. A chance occurrence seems likely given that Joan knew the approximate due date. However, because similar experiences occur so often to people who don't know the mother's expected date of birth or even that she is pregnant, one can't help but think there is more at work here than happenstance.

"I can often feel when a woman is about to go into labor even when she is miles away," admits one obstetrician. "Sometimes I am awakened from a sound sleep with the sudden feeling that a baby is about to be born."

Whatever the cause, this phenomenon may be related to another baffling occurrence. Births tend to occur in clusters. Often the laboring women on a busy maternity unit will all begin to progress in labor at approximately the same time, as if they are responding to a hidden current of energy. Many have commented on this "birth energy," the remarkable force that seems to pulsate like a vibrant living current in the room where a birth takes place. Can the birth energy of one woman actually affect another woman's labor as it seems to affect her family? The answer remains inconclusive. Yet, birth energy does seem to be a real phenomenon many have felt.

As California midwife and lecturer Elizabeth Davis describes, "Attendants often speak of the 'incredible energy in the room' and of feeling 'drawn into the process.' It's as though the birthing woman opens a window on the universal field for others to look through, whence comes the soul of her baby."[5]

USING INTUITION DURING LABOR

An animal's labor will often stop if the mother doesn't feel she is in a safe place to give birth. Similarly, women can unconsciously inhibit their labors. One New York midwife refers to this phenomenon as "fetal retention syndrome." This condition is particularly common in women with a history of abuse in the family and in women torn between career and motherhood. Frequently the mother doesn't realize the cause of her labor's lack of progress. However, using guided imagery to communicate with the preborn may help the mother confront the conflict and initiate labor.

For example, childbirth companion Kristi Ridd was providing labor support for Melanie, a corporate executive, whose labor had just stopped at seven centimeters cervical dilation for no apparent reason.

The usual in-hospital remedy for a flagging labor is the administration of Pitocin, a hormonal solution used to induce or augment labor. Though effective, Pitocin increases the risk of fetal distress, cesarean section, jaundice in the newborn, and almost invariably causes more painful contractions. For these reasons, before resorting to Pitocin, it is almost always preferable to try natural means of getting labor going. Of course, any method of labor augmentation should be used with the approval of a competent health care provider.

Melanie remained stalled at seven centimeters even after Kristi asked her to try several ways to encourage labor's progress, including going outside for a walk, taking a warm shower, and having a light meal. Kristi asked Melanie to sit in an easy chair and ask her baby what was holding her labor back.

Kristi recalls: "When Melanie tried this, she began crying. 'I can't have this baby!' Melanie exclaimed. 'I'll be a terrible parent and hit my children as I was hit by my parents!'"

Her memory of childhood abuse was followed by a flood of emotion that left her torn about becoming a mother. Needless to say, one can't overcome such ambivalence during the short span of labor. Confronting, acknowledging, and accepting her feelings, however, was enough to initiate labor contractions.

"I asked Melanie how she responds when her employees do something she doesn't like," said Kristi. "When she said she reasoned with them, I suggested she could use the same methods as a parent.

"Then I left Melanie alone with her husband to discuss their feelings. When I returned, both parents had been crying. Ten minutes later, Melanie gave birth to a healthy baby girl."

Attuning to the unborn child can sometimes have lifesaving implications. The following story was reported by a midwife who specializes in helping mothers give birth at home.

"One morning at 3:00 A.M., another midwife who was ill phoned me to attend a birth taking place on a dairy farm. Gloria's vital signs were fine. Her cervix was six centimeters dilated, but the baby's head had not firmly settled in the mother's pelvis. Something was wrong.

"Concerned, I asked Gloria to take a deep breath and look at the baby with her mind. Though she thought it was a crazy idea, she tried it. 'What do you see?' I asked.

"'It's all dark down there,' said Gloria. 'I can't get through the wall.'

"Pretend your mind is a laser beam and laser through the wall and tell me what you see.

" 'Bright light at the end of the tunnel!' Gloria suddenly exclaimed.

"Horrified, I was reminded of the light at the end of the tunnel in near-death experiences. I rushed her to the hospital and raced her by wheel chair down the corridor to labor and delivery. The umbilical cord had prolapsed."

An *umbilical cord prolapse* (when the cord precedes the baby's head in the birth outlet) is a grave and fortunately rare complication usually requiring an emergency cesarean. Otherwise, the baby's head depresses the cord, cutting off the oxygen supply and causing death.

This intuition can probably be easily explained. Without realizing it, the midwife may have felt the prolapsed cord when doing the cervical exam. This, in turn, could have caused her to interpret the mother's "bright light at the end of the tunnel" vision as an ominous sign.

But whatever the cause, the intuition saved the baby's life.

REDUCING LABOR PAIN

The guided imagery exercise, "Communicating With Your Unborn Child," helps many mothers like Melanie get in touch with their intuition in order to overcome complications. Guided imagery can also bring about physiological changes during labor. During childbirth, guided imagery exercises such as "The Special Place" and "The Radiant Breath" are very effective in reducing fear, pain, and length of labor.

There are two reasons for this: First, the mother is more right-hemisphere oriented, and, according to Dr. Emmett Miller, a world-renowned pioneer in the field of psychophysiological medicine, guided imagery "translates cognitive information into terms that can activate the right hemisphere and actually help bring about the goal imagined.[6]

Second, guided imagery gives a mother positive suggestion in the language of the right hemisphere: using metaphor at a time when she is especially open to suggestion.

Childbirth companions and other childbirth professionals use "The Radiant Light" as a means of releasing tension and discomfort during labor. To do this, simply imagine that the in breath is a soft, golden radiant light. Imagine that you are breathing this light directly into the area that is tense or uncomfortable. Imagine the tension or discomfort is being massaged away by a million invisible fingers of radiant light.

"The Special Place" is also very effective in triggering relaxation and reducing the discomfort of labor, particularly if this exercise has been practiced during pregnancy. To relax during labor, recall or have your birth partner remind you of the details of your special place.

THE BLOSSOMING FLOWER

One of the most effective guided imagery exercises for releasing blocks in labor and facilitating the childbirth process is an exercise that focuses on opening. "The Blossoming Flower" is an exercise that centers on an image—a blossoming flower—that is an ideal metaphor for the dilating cervix during first stage and the opening birth canal during second. No image better captures the qualities of warmth, beauty, softness, moisture, fragrance, and opening.[7]

During contractions, imagine a blossoming flower. Choose any flower at all—a rose, a tulip, a water lily—as long as it is beautiful. Imagine the flower opening petal by petal, opening, opening, opening, until it is fully in bloom.

You can add as many details to this exercise as you want, such as the shape of the petals, their delicate or bold shading, dewdrops on the flower, fragrance, the sun's rays coaxing the flower to open, and so on. You can also vary the exercise by imagining you are in a beautiful garden or in a field surrounded by hundreds of flowers. You can take a mental journey of the garden or field and choose the most beautiful flower of all. Then imagine that flower blossoming, petal by petal.

Though no one really knows the reasons behind it, many other laboring women have found this exercise effective in treating prolonged or overdue labor—sometimes with amazing results.

Allison, a first-time mother whose labor stopped progressing at six centimeters continued having painful contractions that did not dilate the cervix—a condition called "failure to progress." The patterned breathing exercises she had practiced so diligently in childbirth classes did nothing to help her relax or alleviate her pain.

Finally, her physician recommended Pitocin. However, her own mother, Marianne, was in the room reading about guided imagery at the time.

As a last resort, Marianne suggested Allison try "The Blossoming Flower" exercise. Allison imagined she was in a garden surrounded by hundreds of beautiful flowers. She chose the most beautiful flower in the garden to observe. Then she imagined the flower opening, opening, opening with each contraction.

Allison began to relax, her pain no longer seemed so overwhelming. In addition, her labor took a dramatic change. Much to the surprise of her physician, the cervix dilated rapidly. Allison gave birth to a beautiful baby boy without the need for chemical intervention.

A NEW APPROACH TO CHILDBIRTH

What happens when we meet the mother's emotional as well as physical needs during labor? What occurs when we provide the mother with a setting where she, not a medical professional, is the star of the show? What transpires if we allow the woman's intuition—not just medical procedures—to guide us? What occurs if we flow with rather than fight the laboring mind response?

This is what French physician Dr. Michael Odent did in the special maternity unit of a small hospital in Pithiviers, a town about an hour's drive from Paris. Although he is most well-known for popularizing waterbirth—birth in which the baby is born in warm water—this is a by-product rather than the core of Dr. Odent's work. His approach centers on providing an ideal environment that encourages a laboring woman to attain what he calls "an optimum instinctive state of consciousness."[8]

The birthing room in Hopital General in Pithiviers is designed to relax the mother and help her evoke her intuition. Painted in earth tones, it includes a low-cushioned large bedlike platform where the mother and others, who assist her or share the birth with her, can move freely. If the laboring woman wants, she can go to an adjacent room that houses a custom-made circular sky-blue pool, seven feet in diameter and two-and-a-half-feet deep. The mother has plenty of room to immerse herself completely and change positions as she desires, and two people can move around freely.

Dr. Odent describes this optimal birth environment as a place of privacy, intimacy, calm, with freedom to labor in any position and the presence of someone with whom the woman is emotionally close. It is strangely different than most hospital rooms. Yet, on second glance, there is something familiar about such a setting. It is similar to an environment most would choose for making love.

When we consider the kinship labor and lovemaking share, it shouldn't be surprising to find that the conditions conducive to satisfying lovemaking also contribute to a safe, positive birth experience. These include peace, privacy, comfort, subdued lighting, freedom from disturbances, and a setting where one feels free to let go and react spontaneously.

RECOGNIZING INTUITION: THE KEY TO RECREATING CHILDBIRTH

Recent research may indicate that we need to rethink the way we look at childbirth. A breakthrough study released by the American Medical Association (AMA) on May 1, 1991, revealed that providing emotional support through labor can transform the experience of birth for mother and baby. Researchers found that the presence of a trained labor-support person—a person who remains with the mother throughout to provide emotional support, encouragement, reassurance, and companionship—leads to a dramatic improvement in maternal-infant health. The study, conducted by world-renowned pediatricians John Kennell and Marshall Klaus, involved more than 600 laboring mothers in a Houston hospital. One group had a supportive companion with them through childbirth. Another group did not. The two groups were compared with staggering results. The mothers with supportive companions had significantly shorter labors. They used less pain relief medication and less Pitocin. The cesarean rate was 8 percent compared to 18 percent among those without companions. The rate of forceps deliveries among the companion group was less than one third that of the group that did not have labor support. In addition, the women with companions had healthier babies and fewer postpartum complications.[9]

Science is just beginning to recognize what women have known intuitively for millennia. As Emily, an incisive New York mother and experienced editor, put it after reading this widely quoted medical study about labor support: "This is something anyone who's ever had a baby could have told the scientists *before* the experiment."

Indeed. But why do labor companions have such a dramatic impact on the experience of birth? (Labor companion and childbirth companion are trademarks of the Association of Childbirth Companions.)

Nothing in the pages of modern obstetrics explains why emotional support can reduce labor pain. Yet study after study shows that labor-support providers dramatically reduce childbirth pain and improve the health of mother and baby. In fact, research reveals that a labor-support provider doesn't even have to do anything in particular to affect the mother's labor. His or her very *presence* in the room is enough to reduce the length of labor![10]

Recognizing the benefits of labor support has kindled enthusiasm about professional labor-support providers throughout the United States. As a result, a new profession has come into being. An increasing number of labor-support providers, some professionally trained, some self-trained, have opened private practices.

These new pioneers on the childbirth frontier call themselves by a bewildering array of names, including childbirth companion, labor coach, childbirth assistant, labor assistant, *monitrice* (from a French verb meaning "to watch over"), and even *doula* (which is actually a term for a postpartum assistant from a Greek word meaning "slave"). But under whatever name they call themselves, all labor-support providers have something in common: the unshakable conviction that emotions influence labor, a simple idea, yet as foreign to traditional obstetrics as ritual magic.

According to the Association of Childbirth Companions (ACC), an organization training and certifying labor-support providers, anyone (male or female) who is committed to helping women give birth can learn to be an effective labor-support person. Though some nurses, mid-wives, childbirth educators, massage therapists, social workers, and other health professionals become childbirth companions, no prior medical or educational background of any kind is required. In fact, most trained labor-support persons have no previous experience in childbirth, other than having given birth themselves or perhaps attending a friend's birth. The ability to give emotional support, not medical knowledge, is the essential quality of an effective childbirth companion. A childbirth companion completing ACC training learns a variety of methods to reduce pain and help the mother avoid childbirth complications. These include massage to reduce pain and the chance of tearing during the birth process; relaxation methods during labor; assistance with the mother's chosen labor-coping method, such as guided imagery (visual-ization) or breathing patterns; helping the father better support his mate; and consumer advocacy.

More important, *every labor-support person does something no other health professional does. In most birth settings, he or she is the only person who remains with the parents throughout labor*. Most physicians are usually present only during the final part of labor to assist during the birth. Nurses come and go as the shifts change. The child-birth companion, on the other hand, is a familiar face from the begin-ning to the end of the mother's labor. The emotional support provided, rather than any comfort technique, is, with little doubt, the reason labor-support persons have such a dramatic effect on the health of mother and baby.

Meeting the mother's emotional needs may be at the root of another fact that remains unexplained in terms of medical science: the superior health statistics associated with midwife-assisted births. Midwives have far less education, background, and experience than obstetricians.

In the United States, a *certified nurse midwife* first becomes a registered nurse, then completes a two-year midwifery program. A *direct-entry midwife*, trained through apprenticeship, midwifery school, or a combination of both, often has no nursing background and sometimes far less experience than a certified nurse midwife.

Dutch midwives, for example, have no nursing background. They train in a midwifery school for only three years. Then they observe and participate in births, witnessing complications as well as normal births.

By contrast, obstetricians are medical doctors who have completed medical training, then go on to specialize in obstetrics. Including years of medical school and residency, obstetricians spend on an average of three times as long in training as midwives. They also have all the latest technology immediately available at their fingertips.

One would think this vast difference in training, education, and experience would spell better maternal-infant health statistics by far on the side of the obstetricians. Paradoxically, the very opposite is true. Both lay-trained and university-educated midwives have health statistics superior to those of physicians.

In the Netherlands—the country with the world's lowest infant mortality rate—midwives care for nearly all pregnant and laboring mothers. During the mother's labor, Dutch midwives work with "home helpers," who play a role similar to that of the childbirth companion. The home helper is trained to assist the midwife during labor and to help the mother and infant for ten days after birth, including doing light housekeeping and cooking, in addition to caring for mother and baby.

In Sweden—the nation that ranks second lowest in infant mortality—nearly all mothers, whether or not they have medical problems requiring the additional help of a physician, receive midwifery care.

By comparison, the United States, with its overwhelming percentage of physician-managed hospital births, has one of the highest infant mortality rates in the world!

Two researchers, Deborah Sullivan and Rose Weitz, associate professors of sociology at Arizona State University set out to do an extensive study of home births in Arizona. They wanted to find out why in the world anyone would elect to give birth at home with a lay midwife who had less than three years' training when they could give birth in a hospital with a much more highly trained and skilled obstetrician.

The results of their extensive analysis of over 3,200 births is nothing short of astounding. The perinatal mortality rate (*perinatal* means "around the time of birth") was 2.2 per thousand. This includes three infant deaths resulting from congenital abnormalities that could not have been avoided in any setting with any practitioner. This analysis, state the researchers, "does suggest that there is little, if any, risk involved in choosing midwife-attended out-of-hospital birth in Arizona."[11]

Many assume the superior health outcome associated with midwifery cases results from midwives selecting only low-risk clients, referring those at high risk of pregnancy or labor complications to obstetricians. If this were true, it wouldn't be surprising for midwives to have better health statistics. However, this is a misconception.

Though most midwives specialize in low-risk birth and generally refer the high-risk mother to a physician, research has repeatedly shown that midwifery care has also had a dramatic impact on improving the health of high-risk mothers and babies. Midwives are associated with a reduced incidence of low birth weight, prematurity, and neonatal mortality regardless of whether the mother is at low or high risk of medical complications.

The population of North Central Bronx Hospital, for example, comprises a large percentage of inner-city black and Hispanic mothers, most of whom are at high risk of complications. Medical intervention is at a minimum. Membranes are not artificially ruptured. Pain relief medication is administered in less than 30 percent of births. Pitocin is used to augment labor in only 3 percent of cases, and 85 percent of mothers give birth in a semi-sitting position without stirrups, and forceps are used in less than 3 percent of births.

The prevailing philosophy of the midwives at North Central Bronx Hospital includes providing emotional support for every woman and giving the mother freedom to follow her intuition rather than hospital rules about eating, drinking, and walking around during labor.

Medical statistician David Stewart, Ph.D., points out: "With a population of mothers at considerably higher than average risk, the midwives of North Central Bronx have achieved better maternal and infant outcomes than the rest of New York City, the State of New York in general, and the United States as a whole. There isn't a single hospital in the entire country with populations of similar risk run by doctors with results as good as this one run by midwives."[12]

Many medical studies have revealed similar startling results.[13]

Why do skilled, experienced midwives have such outstanding health statistics? How can midwives often boast of better health statistics than obstetricians? Medical science has never come up with an answer. Yet almost every woman who gives birth intuitively knows the reason. It is, with little doubt, the same reason childbirth companions spell better health for mothers and babies.

Like the childbirth companion, many (but not all) midwives remain with the mother throughout all or a large part of her labor, providing continual nurturing support. This enables the mother to feel more secure, comfortable, and relaxed and therefore to let go and labor more efficiently. Unlike midwives, most obstetricians come in at the last minute to deliver the baby.

In a nutshell, the midwife takes care of more than the mother's body. As a general rule, she or he also meets the mother's emotional needs, which, in turn, influences her labor."[14]

The convincing evidence in favor of midwives does not devalue the role of modern medicine and needed technological intervention. There is no question: technology has saved lives. Nor is it meant to suggest that every woman should give birth at home. Our discussion about midwives implies that a safe birth depends on nurturing the woman's emotional as well as physical needs.

Why? Are the caring emotions of the childbirth companion or the midwife or the physician who remains with the mother through labor somehow transmitted to the baby? Do they somehow radiate a confidence that makes the mother more secure? Do they influence the mother in ways we don't understand to help her through a healthier, easier birth?

Recall that one of the characteristics of the laboring mind response is heightened emotional sensitivity, and several of the other characteristics previously discussed are all associated with greater openness to intuition, even the thoughts of those around the laboring mother.

The laboring mind response gives us a picture of labor not yet taught in medical schools. It explains why meeting the mother's emotional needs is such a vital component of maternity care. Strange as it may seem, until recently obstetrics had nothing to say about the role of emotions in labor despite the knowledge that meeting the mother's emotional needs may hold the keys to a safer birth for mother and baby. Medical texts focus only on the anatomy and physiology of labor.

No one questions that knowing about the anatomy and physiology of childbirth is essential in providing good medical care. Yet it becomes hard to deny there is another side to the birth story. Most American women would probably be stunned to learn that an obstetrician graduates from medical school, goes through internship, completes residency, then becomes an obstetrician without ever witnessing a single labor from beginning to end. During medical training, the medical student or resident occasionally checks on the laboring woman and attends medical procedures but does not actually sit with the woman throughout her labor. As one retired obstetrician puts it: "How can one have a picture of labor without ever witnessing it?"

It certainly takes more than attending university and studying textbooks to get a true picture of the childbirth experience. Science is just beginning to discover that technology without human nurturing during birth can have tragic consequences.

Consider this imbalance from the baby's perspective. What happens when newborn children are taken away from mother to be cared for by health professionals rather than parents? When the beginning of life is treated like a clinical procedure rather than a celebration and miracle? When newborns are offered bottles of commercial infant formula in place of mother's breast?

In the words of West Coast psychologist David Chamberlain, Ph.D., "There will never be enough psychotherapists to heal the unnecessary traumas created by ignorant parents and professionals in their dealings with babies in the womb and at birth."[15]

Even though the health professionals may be in the dark about mothers and babies, even though expectant parents often make choices based on erroneous beliefs, even though medical science is still in its infancy regarding how emotions affect childbirth, our children know how birth should occur.

Priscilla recalls, during an episode of hypnosis, the nightmare of trauma and confusion that too often characterized American birth. "I'm in someone's arms, this woman in white. She's taking me away from my mother! Mother is on the delivery table asleep. She didn't even know. They shouldn't have done it. They took me away!"[16]

Anita, a girl who also vividly recalls the minutes after birth, expresses a similar view: "They handed me to someone, a lady. It's cold. The surroundings are so new, it's frightening. I can't hear my mother, I can't feel my mother; that's frightening. And they took me away."[17]

Charles, another child recalling the minutes after birth, has this to say: "I can't hear anybody, can't feel anybody. It's cold and I don't understand what is happening. In a matter of minutes everything has changed. . . . Before I was born, I was constantly touched or surrounded. Now I'm not being touched at all."

And from Judy, "No one is looking at me, no one is talking to me. Feels like not being alive."[18]

Fortunately, contemporary maternity care is beginning to incorporate emotional support through labor. Childbirth educators are learning about the laboring mind response. American hospitals are eliminating the cold and clinical appearing delivery rooms in favor of homelike labor-delivery-recovery-postpartum rooms, or LDRPs—a single room where the mother and, often, her family remains through the entire childbearing experience.

However, in a few birth facilities, the emphasis is on the place not the person. As Dr. Celeste Philips, former clinical obstetrical specialist for the surgeon general's office and founder of Phillips and Fenwick, a firm specializing in helping hospitals create family-centered maternity care programs, warns: "Look beyond the decorated birthing rooms. What is the philosophy behind those rooms? What does the staff believe about childbirth? It's the people that create good obstetrical care, the people and what they believe."

Professor of nursing, Susan McKay, Ph.D., agrees: "If the humanization of the birth process is to be achieved, the birth environment must encompass far more than an attractive physical appearance. The assertion commonly made about LDRPs is that they provide humanistic childbirth—which ignores the truth that people, not rooms, create humanistic care."[19]

It is hoped that, a humanistic approach to birth will one day describe every hospital, every childbearing center, every birthing environment throughout the world.

In light of the laboring mind response, two major components are essential to a safe, positive birth: an environment where the mother feels she can let go and spontaneously react to her intuition and nurturing health care providers.

The remarkable effect labor support has in creating a more rewarding birth, the safety of midwifery care, and guided imagery's power to reduce the fear, pain, and even length of labor all have something in common. They all presuppose that some force—call it a type of energy—affects the mother and her baby during the childbearing process.

This energy has always remained a mystery—perhaps the greatest mystery. It has never been measured in a laboratory or viewed on a monitor screen. Yet, it probably remains the single most important factor in creating safer, more rewarding birth. It is so powerful that just feeling it in the same room where a woman labors can influence uterine function, causing a shorter, easier labor. And it is so close to home, so obvious, that it is a marvel that a century of obstetrics has failed to consider it.

The power that best enables the mother to give birth in the most rewarding way possible may be something quite familiar, the same force that put the baby in the womb in the very beginning. Love. Which may itself be a paranormal phenomenon.

ESP: THE BOND OF LOVE

Love, the most basic of human feelings. How is love communicated? We know the many ways we communicate love to our children. But let's briefly return to the child in utero. Studies have repeatedly shown that expectant mothers who feel love and acceptance for their developing baby are more likely to have healthier, more contented infants.

Yet, speaking of love and acceptance, Toronto psychiatrist Thomas Verny points out: "*Nothing we know about the human body explains why these feelings affect the unborn child.* Yet study after study show that happy contented women are far more likely to have bright outgoing infants."[20] That such thoughts and feelings *are* conveyed from parent to child "tends," as Dr. Verny suggests, "to bear out the theory of extrasensory communication in the young."

Which suggests the paranormal may be an integral part of a love bond all parents and children share.

Pioneer pediatricians Marshall Klaus and John Kennell observed species-specific behavior in the development of parent-infant attachment.[21] Though the bonding process begins while the baby is in utero, Drs. Klaus and Kennell have noted a sensitive period during the first hour after birth. This is usually a period of high energy for the mother, father, and baby. The baby is usually exceptionally alert for an hour or so before sleeping deeply for another three or four hours. During this time the mother "takes in" and receives her child.

Studies show that the bonding process is "species-specific," that is, members of any one given species pretty much follow the same pattern. The human mother usually touches and explores her baby in a predictable pattern: first exploring the baby's head and extremities with her fingertips, then caressing the trunk with her open palm, and finally enfolding the baby in her arms.

The parent-baby dyad is so closely linked that from the first day of life the newborn moves in precise and sustained motions that are synchronous with the structure of adult speech.[22]

An astounding film made by psychiatrist Daniel Stern of Cornell University shows a baby held in her father's arms. When viewed in slow motion, the film shows the father's head beginning to move down as the baby's head begins to move up to meet him. Similarly when the father's right hand begins to move up from his side, the baby's left arm, begins to move at the same time. The opposite hands of father and baby then come together over the baby's middle where the baby clasps her father's finger and falls asleep.

This phenomenon is called "entrainment." Drs. Louis Sander and William Condon of the Child Development Unit of Boston University Medical Center studied this synchrony. They found that the motions of all body parts, including the infants' eyes, brow, mouth, head, elbows, shoulders, hips, and feet were coordinated with the syllables of adult speech. Moreover, American infants synchronized to language spoken in Chinese as well as in English. Yet meaningless sounds did not elicit this reaction! Drs. Sander and Condon speculate that entrainment may be linked to the bond between human beings.[23]

A group of pediatricians and engineers joined forces to do a complex computer analysis further exploring entrainment at Aiiku Hospital in Japan. They videotaped an infant's body motions down to the microsecond while the mother talked with the baby. The infant moved in harmony with his mother's speech and the mother talked to her infant by reacting to the baby's body movements. Yet when the researchers made tapping noises and other sounds, they found no relationship between the infant's movements and the nonhuman sounds.[24]

In another study, researchers found a correspondence between cry patterns of premature babies born at only five months' gestation and the intonations and rhythms of the mother's speech. This adds to the evidence that babies acquire the mother's accents and speech sounds during early prenatal development.[25]

After birth, parent and baby's incredible rapport continues. Many parents sense the unseen connection with their children throughout life.

The breast-feeding relationship may be an extension of the seemingly extrasensory rapport mother and child shared in utero. Nature designed immediate postbirth breast-feeding as a delicate symbiotic relationship benefiting both mother and baby. When the baby suckles at the breast, the pituitary gland releases the hormone oxytocin. This causes the uterus to contract and deliver the placenta. Once the placenta is delivered, oxytocin helps keep the uterine muscles clamped tightly around the open blood vessels at the placental site, preventing postpartum hemorrhage. At the same time, the newborn receives the first milk called *colostrum*, rich in vitamins, nutrients, and antibodies to many viral and bacterial diseases, helping to prevent infections.

Mother and baby become so attuned during breast-feeding that milk production and secretion automatically respond to the baby's crying. The sound of the baby's crying stimulates the pituitary gland to secrete oxytocin, which in turn triggers the milk ejection (let-down) reflex. Lactation experts agree that the let-down reflex is a physiological reaction to either the physical stimulus of suckling or a psychological stimulus, such as hearing the baby's cry or thinking about the baby.

However, there may be another, hitherto unexplored dimension of the let-down reflex. Could this universal maternal reflex also be a reaction to a parapsychological stimulus? Mothers who are away from the baby, shopping or on another errand, have noticed a sudden let-down of milk at a time when the baby would ordinarily be feeding. It is not uncommon for the mother to later discover that the baby woke at the time her milk let down.

For example, Julie, a new breast-feeding mother, reports: "I started back to work this week. Suddenly, my milk let down spontaneously and painfully at 12:30 P.M. When I picked my baby up, and got the information sheet his caregiver keeps on his activities, I found he had been given a bottle at 12:30."

Terry, a new father recalls hearing his newborn son cry when the child was miles distant in the hospital. He reports: "Our son was born on October 12, 1982, early in the evening. I went home about midnight, and awoke at five the next morning to the sound of a baby crying. Seconds later, my wife called from the hospital. She said that the nurse had just taken the baby away from her, and that he was crying terribly.

" 'I know,' I told her."

And to think, this extraordinary rapport begins in the cradle of human life: the womb.

CHAPTER 10

DEVELOPING YOUR INTUITION

Following are guidelines and exercises for enhancing the intuitive voice. They are derived from a wide variety of experts in the field of developing intuition, including parapsychologists, psychologists, hypnotherapists, business executives, health professionals, and others who use intuition in their daily lives.

GETTING ACQUAINTED WITH YOUR INTUITION

Getting to know the voice within can both open the door on a new way of looking at the world and enrich daily life. Intuition is a lifelong mode of knowing that can lead to a fuller, more rewarding way of relating to your children and the world around you.

Enhancing intuition can lead to a sense of oneness with all life and the creative life force, awakening a transpersonal awareness. At the same time, intuition can lead to a healthier life, perhaps even warning parents of possible health complications with their child.

BASIC GUIDELINES FOR ENHANCING INTUITION

Intuition is wholly unpredictable.

"There is no single diet, life-style, or other habit that will magically increase or decrease your intuition," says psychiatrist and parapsychological researcher Berthold Schwarz. "What works for one person as a intuition-conducive lifestyle may not affect another."

BENEFITS OF DEVELOPING INTUITION

Combining intuition with rational thought can give you a broader perspective on everything from birth to business. Here are just a few of the benefits of developing intuition:

- Assisting decision making
- Solving problems
- Warning about health problems
- Inspiring creative activities
- Awakening a transpersonal awareness

People who have intuitive experiences (including gifted psychics) frequently offer conflicting advice about enhancing intuition. Some prescribe vegetarian diets; others insist on avoiding alcohol or so-called recreational drugs; still others recommend adopting a certain life-style free from the influence of industrial or chemical pollutants. Dr. Schwarz considers all of these recommendations "prissy preconceptions." There is no proof any of them heightens intuition. A lifestyle that is comfortable for one intuitive person may do nothing to help another enhance latent abilities.

Though there is no way to guarantee an intuitive experience, you can take a number of steps to increase the likelihood of intuition. You may find some or all of the following suggestions helpful in awakening your own intuition.

Value your intuition. The first step in developing intuition is to appreciate this little understood way of knowing. Intuition is like a neurotically sensitive houseguest. The slightest criticism and he runs and hides. Valuing your intuition, paying attention to it, and giving importance to this nonrational means of knowing is often enough to awaken it. This may be one reason why midwives, as a general rule, tend to be more intuitive than most other health professionals. In addition to being in continual contact with pregnant women whose intuition almost seems to spill over and affect others, most midwives value the mother's inner feelings. Physicians, on the other hand, tend to report fewer intuitive episodes though they also work with expectant mothers. Whereas midwives center on the mother's inner life in addition to her physical changes, most medical doctors tend to view pregnancy and birth through clinical eyes. Of course, this is only a general rule. Some physicians work with the heart of a midwife and some midwives have an entirely clinical orientation. No single profession (aside from that of professional psychic) can claim a corner on intuition.

Believe in your intuition. Believing in intuition goes hand in hand with valuing the intuitive voice. Parapsychological researchers have proved this point with a battery of rigorous tests. In one oft-quoted experiment, psychologists Gertrude Schmeidler and R. A. McConell of City College of New York separated 1,157 students into two groups: the sheep—that is, those who believed in ESP—and the goats—those who didn't believe. She gave both groups identical ESP testing. Not surprisingly, the sheep scored significantly higher than the goats. Among parapsychologists, this has become known appropriately as the "sheep-goat effect."[1] Dr. Charles Tart, professor of psychology at the University of California at Davis, did a similar experiment, dividing groups into sheep and goats and testing them for ESP. The sheep consistently scored above chance, while the goats scored below.

Pay attention to hunches and gut reactions. Intuition is frequently so undramatic that it virtually passes unnoticed or is often forgotten immediately after the episode. Intuition often comes as a subtle change in consciousness. You may have a sense of being more alert or even more "tuned in." Paying attention to these subtle feelings may help to awaken intuition. Becoming aware of intuition is similar to recalling dreams immediately upon waking. People who say they dream infrequently or can't remember dreams often begin experiencing more vivid dreams after making an attempt to recall them. Likewise, making an effort to notice your inner voice may bring more intuitive experiences to mind. You may want to practice paying daily attention to your intuition. To enhance this, if you are of a writing turn of mind, you might even want to keep a journal.

Adopt a watchful alert state. People who rely on their intuition in their daily lives recommend cultivating a *watchful alert*, but not a judgmental state. One way of doing this is by becoming aware of your thoughts and feelings without trying to do anything about them. Allowing some of these feelings to "just be there" and following them without responding may lead to intuition. The watchful alert state is especially useful when using guided imagery exercises to further develop your intuition and healing abilities.

Act on your intuition. Like any other skill, intuition improves with practice. Acting on intuition and discovering your insights were correct may give you the confidence to expand your intuitive awareness. For example, a midwife had a fleeting but distinct feeling she should phone one of her clients prior to leaving on a two-hour trip to the beach, where she would be away from her phone. She called and was surprised to find her client was in labor. Of course there is a big, but not always easily recognized, difference between acting on a hunch and impulsive behavior. Needless to say, one should think through major decisions in the light of the rational mind before taking actions. Top executives who consciously use their intuition to guide their most important decisions recognize how vital it is to act on intuition. As Professor Agor, director of the Master in Public Administration Program at the University of Texas at El Paso, reports: "They identified a specific body of cause or indications employed as guideposts for action, and this process has resulted by their own admission in every successful major decision. At the same time, they stated that their mistakes resulted primarily from the fact that they failed to use their intuition effectively to guide their decisions. They allowed themselves to get 'off course' by letting such factors as ego involvement block the signals normally picked up by their intuitive radar."[2] Acting on your intuition sometimes leads to a sense of well-being and an inner certainty of doing the right thing. The more you are able to act on your intuition, the more likely your intuitive voice will grow.

Integrate your intuition with rational thinking. Though a passive alert state is conducive to intuition, it is wise to later analyze your insights with the logic of the rational mind. The ideal goal is integrating intuition with rational thought, so that both entirely different modes of knowing work in harmony.

Use whatever method works best for enhancing your intuition. You can use any of a wide variety of methods to awaken intuition. Some find that intuition occurs most naturally while meditating. Others find their intuition flows while jogging or at some other physical activity. Some will find guided imagery most effective in enhancing the intuitive voice. Others find it effective simply to turn inward and center their energy on intuition.

Cultivate friends or a support group that values intuition. One of the most detrimental blocks in the development of intuition is the criticism of skeptical people who don't appreciate intuitive means of knowing. This is especially true when you're first developing your intuitive voice and may feel insecure about whether your intuition is valid. One executive who uses intuition in his business has this to say: "I share this fact easily with other friendly intuitive people, but try to disguise it as careful planning, research, or an intellectual effort around others. This is not a matter of adopting a cunning strategy; those without the willingness/ability to use their own intuition are often frightened by intuitive demonstrations or reject any evidence not fitting their current paradigm. It's hard, however, for anyone to talk about intuition—we lack theory that also fits our rational body of knowledge."[3] Others who value their intuition can lend invaluable support while you are trying to get in touch with your own inner resources.

SYMBOLS OF INTUITION

Gifted psychics frequently associate a particular symbol with the dawn of the intuitive state of mind. The symbol—either a mythic image or a self-created symbol—seems to become a metaphor for the intuitive voice. Such symbols include a third eye (symbolizing second sight), a bird in flight, or other object.

Others who are developing their intuition may also notice that a particular symbol appears again and again. A symbol of intuition is often a personal metaphor that may appear to have no clearly understood meaning. For example, every time I enter a passive relaxed state of mind I associate with intuition, I see a bell in my mind's eye. The bell is like a fleeting image in the corner of my mind. The bell image is continually transformed. One day it looks like a church bell, another I see the bell from a different angle, or just the clapper and one side of the bell. Sometimes the bell appears to be something that would fit in a jewelry box, at others it looks like it would outsize all but the sturdiest belfry. But however it appears and from whatever angle, it is always a bell. At first I didn't associate it with anything special. But after the symbol kept appearing, I began associating it with intuition.

Not everyone experiences a symbol of intuition. However, if you do glimpse such a symbol, it may fleetingly appear at the corner of your mind prior to an intuitive experience. If a symbol spontaneously appears and you begin to associate it as a metaphor of your intuition, you may be able to invoke the intuitive voice by imagining that symbol.

EXERCISES FOR ENHANCING INTUITION

Sometimes called visualization, guided imagery is a means of translating positive thoughts into dynamic mental pictures or images. Guided imagery exercises can bring about a state of deep physical and mental relaxation, ideal for developing intuition.

GUIDELINES FOR USING GUIDED IMAGERY

Follow these guidelines for best results in developing intuition:

- Use guided imagery with relaxation methods that incorporate suggestion in the exercise, such as "Autogenic Stress Release" and "The Radiant Light."
- Play relaxing background music. Though familiar music can be relaxing, if it is associated with strong memories, it may prove counterproductive and distract you from the exercise. Consider music you use only for the exercise. After repeated sessions with the same music, the music may elicit relaxation.
- Allow ample time for each exercise. Ten to thirty minutes should be sufficient.
- Practice guided imagery in a dimly lit room where you are unlikely to be disturbed.
- Remove belt, shoes, glasses.
- Adopt the position of your choice. Some find sitting up in a cross-legged position conducive to relaxation; others are best able to relax when lying down. Many people prefer lying flat on the back. This position should be avoided, however, during late pregnancy because pressure from the heavy uterus on an artery from the heart (vena cava) interferes with blood circulation. Other positions include side-lying, semireclining, or even sitting in an easy chair.
- Read through the entire exercise. Get familiar with the steps. They are easy to remember with a little practice.
- Make a tape of the exercise, perhaps with the background music of your choice, and play it back when you are ready to begin the exercise.

RELAXATION EXERCISES

Before beginning guided imagery, try "Autogenic Stress Release," "The Radiant Light," or another relaxation exercise of your choice. You may find that varying relaxation exercises with each session keeps your mind alert.

AUTOGENIC STRESS RELEASE

The following exercise was developed in the 1920s by Dr. J. H. Schultz, a German psychiatrist, as part of a process called Autogenic Therapy. It brings about relaxation of body and mind with the use of suggestion.

To begin, sit in a dimly lit, quiet room in a comfortable position, where you can begin to relax. Become aware of your breathing . . . letting your breath come and go in its own natural rhythm. As you observe your breathing, let your breath become just a little deeper, a little slower, without straining or forcing the breath in any way . . . a little deeper, a little slower.

Be aware of the breath you take in, letting the breath enter your body effortlessly. Notice the slight pause between the breath you take in and the breath you let out. Be aware of the breath you let out, letting the breath leave your body slowly. Notice the slight pause before your next breath in and let the pause become just a little longer. Continue to breathe in this deep, rhythmic, relaxing way throughout this exercise.

With each breath in and with each breath out, mentally repeat to yourself the following words: my right arm is heavy and warm . . . my right arm is heavy and warm . . . my right arm is heavy and warm. Now, with each breath in and out, mentally repeat: my left arm is heavy and warm . . . my left arm is heavy and warm . . . my left arm is heavy and warm.

With each breath in and each breath out, mentally repeat: my right leg is heavy and warm . . . my right leg is heavy and warm. Now, with each breath in and out, repeat: my left leg is heavy and warm . . . my left leg is heavy and warm.

With each breath in and each breath out, tell yourself: my pelvic organs are warm, relaxed, and comfortable . . . my pelvic organs are warm, relaxed, and comfortable. Continue to breathe deeply and slowly.

With the next breath out, mentally repeat: It breathes me . . . it breathes me.

With each breath out, say to yourself: the muscles of my back and neck are warm and relaxed . . . the muscles of my back and neck are warm and relaxed. Now, with each breath out, mentally say: my jaw muscles are loose and relaxed . . . my jaw muscles are loose and relaxed.

With each breath out, repeat: my forehead is quiet and cool . . . my forehead is quiet and cool. Now, with each breath out, repeat: my eyelids are relaxed and heavy . . . my eyelids are relaxed and heavy.

Enjoy the sensation of complete relaxation for a few minutes. When you are ready to return to the world of your everyday waking life, take a deep breath, slowly count to five, and open your eyes.

THE RADIANT LIGHT

"The Radiant Light" is one of the easiest and most effective exercises to use for relaxation, healing, and enhancing your intuition. This exercise can be used at any time, either by itself or in combination with guided imagery exercises to develop intuition.

For relaxation, do the exercise, "The Special Place" or "Autogenic Stress Release." To enhance your intuition, do the exercise, then imagine the light is life energy awakening your intuition. You may want to imagine the radiant light sweeping up and down your body, from head to toe. As you do this, give yourself some positive suggestions, such as "I am becoming more intuitive," or "I am becoming aware of my intuitive voice."

To begin, imagine that with each breath you take in, you are breathing in a soft, golden, radiant light. You can think of this light however you want: as real—life energy—or as imaginary—a metaphor for your breath, whichever you prefer. As you observe your breathing, let your breath become just a little deeper, a little slower, without straining or forcing the breath in any way . . . a little deeper, a little slower. Continue to breathe in this deep, rhythmic, relaxing way throughout this exercise.

With each breath in, imagine that this light is filling your body. With each breath out, imagine tension flowing away. With your next breath in, imagine the radiant light filling the region of your head. With your next few breaths out, imagine all the tension releasing from your scalp, face, and jaw. With each breath out, imagine your jaw loose and relaxed.

As you exhale, imagine the space between your eyebrows growing wider. Imagine all the muscles of your neck relaxing.

With the next breath in, imagine the radiant light filling your back. As you exhale, imagine all the tension flowing away from your back and your back becoming warm and relaxed.

With the next breath in, imagine the radiant light filling your left arm. As you exhale, imagine any tension flowing away—out through the fingertips of your left hand.

With the next breath in, imagine the radiant light filling your right arm. As you exhale, imagine any tension flowing away—out through the fingertips of your right hand. With your next breath in, imagine the radiant light filling your abdomen. Now, as you breathe out, imagine all the tension flowing away from your abdominal region, your abdominal wall relaxing.

With the next breath in, imagine radiant light filling your pelvis with its soft golden radiance. As you exhale, imagine the tension flowing away—out through your pelvic floor, feeling the pelvic floor muscles become relaxed and limp.

With the next breath in, imagine the radiant light filling your left leg. As you exhale, imagine any tension flowing away—out through the sole of your left foot.

With the next breath in, imagine the radiant light filling your right leg. As you exhale, imagine any tension flowing away—out through the sole of your right foot.

Now gently bring your attention back to your head. With the next few breaths in and out, imagine the radiant light sweeping down and up your body from your head to your toes. Dwell on this image for as long as you like. Then, when you are ready to return to your everyday life, count slowly to five, stretch gently and open your eyes.

Another way to do this exercise is to awaken telepathic rapport between you and your mate, family member, close friend, or child.

TELEPATHIC RAPPORT

Experts in the field of parapsychology recommend that people who are trying to develop a telepathic rapport synchronize their breath with one another. Likewise, imagining that you are breathing in harmony with your mate and baby may accomplish similar results in your family.

If you'd like to try developing a telepathic rapport with another person—your mate, health care provider, or friend—try the following exercise. Verify the results later for accuracy, if you wish.

DEVELOPING TELEPATHIC RAPPORT

First, do "The Radiant Light" exercise. Then imagine that the soft, glowing, radiant light surrounding you is also surrounding your child, your mate, a friend.

Once this image is in mind, attempt to "send a message." Choose any message you want. You send an image, a thought, or a feeling. Or, you could select a picture of a person, place, or object that has some emotional meaning to you and send this image.

RUNNING ENERGY

An exercise Elizabeth Davis recommends in her book *Women's Intuition* is "Running Energy." This exercise both inspires her intuition and assists her through her often stressful midwifery practice when she finds herself staying up through the night.[4]

You may want to combine "Running Energy" with "The Radiant Light."

To begin, be aware of the energy inside you. Notice how if feels. You may want to imagine this energy as a soft radiant light. Let the energy begin to course through you, flowing with your breath. You can imagine this energy flowing up and down from the soles of your feet to your head, sweeping over and through your entire body.

Now imagine the energy expanding. Imagine it reaching beyond the limits of your body, expanding outward to fill the space around you. Feel a sense of being connected to everything around you. Enjoy the energy flowing through you as long as you want. Then, when you are ready to return to the world of your everyday waking life, take a deep breath, slowly count to five, and open your eyes.

THE SPECIAL PLACE

In the following exercise, you create your own personal inner sanctuary based on a real or imaginary place that you associate with relaxation, comfort, security, and peace. This is one of the most basic and popular relaxation exercises. However, you can also use this powerful guided imagery to awaken your intuition by asking yourself a question while you are in your special place or by combining it with another exercise, such as "The Cottage."

When you are relaxed, body and mind, imagine that you are in a very special place that makes you feel comfortable, relaxed, secure, and at peace. It can be any place at all, real or imaginary—a room in your home, a cabin in the mountains, a corner of your yard, the warm sand of the beach where you can hear the ocean waves rolling to shore, an open meadow clothed with wild flowers, a moss-carpeted spot in a woodland grove near a bubbling brook—anywhere you feel relaxed, comfortable, secure, and at peace.

Take a few minutes to explore your special place. Notice the details. You may notice that the more you explore the details, the more clear and vivid your special place becomes. Meanwhile, if irrelevant thoughts enter your mind, let them drift away like puffy, white clouds carried by the breeze on a clear spring day. As you enjoy feeling relaxed in your special place, ask yourself a question, any question to which you want an answer. Then, allow your mind to be still.

Let thoughts, feelings, and images drift into your mind. Don't try to analyze what comes to mind. You can always do that later. For now, just let the thoughts, feelings, or images be there. Continue to explore and enjoy your special place. As you do so, acknowledge that this is your very own place. No one can enter without your invitation. But you can return here any time you want to feel relaxed, comfortable, secure, and at peace.

When you are ready to return to your everyday life, take a few deep breaths, stretch gently, and open your eyes, feeling refreshed and revitalized.

MEETING YOUR INTUITIVE SELF

To enhance the development of intuition, try this exercise. Though it is similar to "The Special Place," some may find this easier to use. Remember to try a variety of exercises and see which ones work best for you.

The following adaptation of Elizabeth Davis's exercise works equally well for health professionals and lay persons.[5]

MEETING YOUR INTUITION

Choose a place and position that are relaxing to you. Then close your eyes, and sense the room around you.

Now imagine getting up and walking outside. Be aware of your movements. Feel as though you are actually doing this.

Now imagine yourself in a place that is beautiful or somehow special to you, a place you've been to before or one that springs from your imagination. Bring yourself fully into this environment.

And now, emerging from the scene, allow an image of your knowingness, your wise, intuitive self appears. He or she may appear as a different person or a slightly altered double of you—either is fine.

When you are ready, ask your intuitive self if he or she has anything to tell you. You might want to take his or her hand and feel the connection between you. When you are ready, say farewell and watch your intuitive self depart. Let the scene fade, and bring yourself back into the room again, and open your eyes.

Now take a moment to contemplate the nature of your intuitive self. Did your intuitive self say anything you know in your heart to be true? Had he or she qualities you've thought missing (or deeply buried) in you?

Don't be concerned if you don't immediately see results or if you have difficulty visualizing your intuitive self. The intuitive self is a metaphor for your inner voice. This exercise is one way to help you attune to that inner voice. You may or may not visualize a distinct image.

THE COTTAGE

"The Cottage" encompasses a common but powerful image for both relaxation and connecting with intuition: traveling down a long stairway and entering a room or home. The journey down the stairway is a symbol of relaxation, each step down, relaxing mind and body more and more.

You can think of the cottage as the domain of your intuition. You may even associate what you see beyond the door with a *symbol of intuition*. You can do this exercise either by itself or in combination with "The Special Place." If you do the two exercises together, first do "The Special Place," then proceed with "The Cottage." You may want to imagine that the stairway begins somewhere within your personal inner sanctuary.

Once you are in a comfortable position in a dimly lit room and your mind and body are relaxed, imagine you are descending a long staircase. Imagine that each step down brings you to a deeper, more relaxed state of body and mind. You may even want to count the steps in reverse order as you descend, beginning with ten and ending with zero.

At the bottom of the stairs, imagine a cottage before you. Imagine that the door is closed. Imagine someone brings you the key to the door. Picture yourself opening the door and entering the cottage. Take a while to explore the inside of the cottage. Notice the details. You may find that the more you explore the details, the more clear and vivid they become.

Spend as long as you like in the cottage. When you have enjoyed being in the cottage, go back through the door and up the stairs, slowly, one step at a time. Tell yourself that you can return to this place anytime you choose. When you are ready to return to the world of your everyday waking life, count slowly to five, stretch gently, and open your eyes.

USING INTUITION IN DECISION MAKING

At any time of life, intuition can enable you to solve problems and make wise decisions based on a combination of insight and logic. Sometimes, one must make a decision under pressure—for example, whether to seek emergency medical care. Other times, you'll have plenty of time for more leisurely decision-making. Needless to add, intuition should never replace competent medical care.

The following steps will enable you to invoke intuition when making decisions:

- *First,* clarify the question or problem. A vague and hazy question is unlikely to elicit a clear answer. Think the question through in the light of your rational mind before posing it to your intuition.
- *Second,* get into a relaxed state of body and mind and ask your inner self the question. To do this, you can use "The Special Place" guided imagery exercise. Once you are in your personal inner sanctuary, ask the question.
- *Third,* relax and allow your mind to remain open to thoughts, images, and impressions that may arise in answer to your question. Remain in a passive alert state without judging the thoughts or images that come to mind. Just allow them to be there and observe.
- *Fourth,* don't be concerned if nothing comes to mind in response to the question you've posed during this exercise. This is perfectly normal. In the course of daily life, you may think of an answer to your question hours, even days, later.
- *Fifth,* when and if you receive an answer, analyze it in the light of common sense. If it seems right, act on it. Needless to say, it does little good to seek an intuitive solution to a problem without the willingness to act on it.

For example, while doing "The Special Place," Carol, a first-time mother, asked her inner self what she most needed in order to have a safe and rewarding birth. Almost immediately, the intuition flashed into her mind telling her she should change her physician and hospital. Since this decision required giving up the benefits of her health insurance in the face of a personal economic struggle she was already experiencing, she discussed it with her husband, Paul, and weighed her options. Her physician, it turned out, had a 30 percent cesarean rate. Fortunately, for her and her baby, she decided to follow her intuition. After the baby was born, she was grateful for her decision. As she put it: "It would have been impossible to experience such a peaceful birth if Dan and I hadn't bitten the bullet and changed doctors."

TESTING YOUR INTUITION

Test your intuition if you find it helpful. If you are interested in testing and developing your ESP in the rigorous controlled manner employed by parapsychologists, use an updated parapsychological text.

Dry as dust parapsychological experiments are important from a scientific point of view to validate intuition. They enable you to isolate and identify genuine extrasensory perception. However, in daily life, learning to value intuition is of greater importance.

Bear in mind that many intuitive experiences cannot be validated. It is near impossible, for example, to quantify and verify the feeling of communicating with a child if the child is very young or even as yet unborn. Moreover, all intuitive experiences are not necessarily paranormal. In fact, the majority may be based on subliminal feelings. The intuition, however, is no less valuable.

CHAPTER 11

INTUITION THAT OPENS DOORS

A Japanese physician has finished examining an expectant mother. Her nutritional habits have been poor, and her baby has not been gaining adequate weight. Rather than lecturing her on better nutrition, the doctor dims the lights in the examining room and leaves her alone for twenty minutes to do an exercise.

The exercise, is "Communicating With Your Unborn Child," is the same guided imagery introduced in chapter 6. While doing the exercise to tap her inner resources, the mother will silently ask her baby a question: "What do you most need right now?"

When the obstetrician returns, the expectant mother is deeply relaxed, peaceful. She has made a decision that will affect the future health of her baby. "My baby needs me to change my diet," she says. Her discovery of the need to change her diet seems only so much common sense to us. However, for her it was a breakthrough.

This exercise is one way an expectant parent or health professional can use intuition for better maternal-child health. Throughout this book, we've discussed many other ways intuition occurs during the childbearing months.

Can the mother, the father, the health professional tap into these intuitive experiences for an easier, safer childbirth? Can medical science tap this inexplicable means of knowing during pregnancy and even the labor process itself?

Yes. Without question, parents and health professionals alike can incorporate many forms of intuition in daily life for a healthier pregnancy and healthier baby. Paying greater attention to intuitive flashes and using intuitive exercises may also prove to be a useful diagnostic, warning parents and professionals of impending complications before they can be detected by medical tests. Intuition can also help parents come to terms with emotional trauma, ranging from their own birth and prenatal experiences to the trauma suffered from pregnancy loss. In addition, we can use intuition in a wide variety of ways to facilitate healing. And finally, paying greater attention to intuition can help us create health care conducive to safer, easier births.

WAYS INTUITION CAN AFFECT CHILDBEARING

Both parents and health professionals can turn to intuition to do all of the following:

- Detect complications
- Resolve complications
- Resolve emotional conflicts
- Heal
- Create an easier, safer birth

DETECTING AND RESOLVING COMPLICATIONS

Childbirth professionals often find themselves becoming more intuitive as they work with pregnancy and birth. It is almost as if the intuitive ability of the expectant mother were able to influence and affect those around her. Some childbirth professionals combine their intuition with their clinical knowledge and other means of diagnosing.

For example, Laurine Kingston, a midwife in Bennion, Utah, says: "I use a combination of clinical skills, sight, body language, and intuition in my practice. I feel as if a little package is placed inside of the client at the time of conception. In that package is a total pattern of how that person is going to be and what is going to happen. That is what I try to see with intuition. Intuition helps me enhance the miracle of birth for my clients."

However, Laurine's intuition didn't come automatically. "I've fine tuned my intuition over the years," she says.

USING EMPATHY IN HEALTH CARE

Telesomatic symptoms and subliminal perception of a client's symptoms can help health practitioners provide better health care by doing the following:

- Informing the client that his or her symptoms may really be a reflection of the symptoms of another. The most common example of this is father-felt pregnancy symptoms.

- Sensing symptoms in the health care provider's own body and using this to corroborate other more traditional means of diagnosis.

- Letting empathetic symptoms guide the health care provider in providing more nurturing care. For example, a midwife often develops a rapport with her client and can sense in her own body where the mother feels discomfort and massage that area of her client.

Another way to detect complications and provide better health care is with "ESP of the body." In chapter 4, we discussed how fathers sometimes experience their mate's symptoms. Frequently this results from a type of ESP called a *telesomatic symptom*. Despite several intriguing experiments and many case histories leaving no doubt as to the reality of telesomatic symptoms, there is little in medical literature about the practical, down-to-earth value of telesomatic symptoms."[1] Yet, the implications in health care are tremendous.

Accepting telesomatic symptoms—however inexplicable—as normal can help health professionals better diagnose and reassure clients. Professor of psychiatry Ian Stevenson, of the University of Virginia, Richmond expresses the need to pay more attention to what may be psi-mediated physiological symptoms. "It seems quite possible that many experiences of the paranormal communication of pain or other physical symptoms occur and fail to attract the attention they deserve or be properly interpreted."[2]

Dr. Stevenson continues: "It is worth pointing out that if a person [who is] sensitive to paranormal communications and liable to their expression in the form of pain or other physical symptoms has repeated episodes of such symptoms . . . [,which have] no other obvious genesis, the patient may be unjustly accused of being hypochondriacal."[3]

In analyzing thirty-five cases of telepathic impressions, Dr. Stevenson found that "fourteen percipients had definite physical symptoms during the impression experience. Four of these felt so ill or weak that they thought they were going to die. Four percipients developed pain, and in two of these pain cases the agent was having labor pains at the time of the experience."[4]

Health professionals can sometimes sense the physical symptoms of a client, a process known as *empathy*.

Dr. B. A. Ruggieri, M.D., reports a fascinating account of a telesomatic symptom he experienced while examining a thirteen-and-a-half-year-old girl with temporal lobe epilepsy. Dr. Ruggieri experienced a "severe but momentary abdominal cramp. The thought went through my mind, 'I hope she does not get a spell,' since her convulsive disorder frequently manifested itself as abdominal epilepsy. I had experienced the cramp as my own but mentally associated it [with] my patient's problems. Immediately thereafter this girl began to stare straight ahead and make swallowing movements. When it was over, she described her feelings: "It felt as though my stomach was about to blow up." Later when the daughter described this incident to the mother, the latter asked, 'Did you tell the doctor you had this spell?' and the girl reportedly answered, 'I didn't have to, he sensed it.' "[5]

One retired physician often felt cramping in his abdomen when a client, sometimes many miles distant, began her labor. The cramping would be so intense that it frequently woke him from a sound sleep, usually minutes before the telephone rang, with the mother announcing her labor under way! Over the course of time, he began to connect the cramping with the phone call that soon followed. Eventually, when he woke with cramps, he got up and dressed, prepared for the inevitable phone call!

When feeling the physical symptoms of another is out-of-control, it can become a problem. Several midwives have reported that a client's labor contractions triggered the onset of their own menstrual periods. Dr. Trethowan, a psychiatrist, reports of a midwife "who had to change her occupation because attendance at confinements seemed to cause her to suffer attacks of abdominal colic."[6]

Symptoms so pronounced that they cause one to change profession are unusual. In fact, health professionals who develop empathy attempt to learn to perceive the physical symptoms of another without actually taking on the symptoms.

A few midwives experience their client's symptoms in the course of their daily practice. In her busy practice, California midwife Elizabeth Davis frequently feels the experience of laboring women. "By making physical contact with the mother (holding her shoulders or her feet) and opening myself fully, I could feel in my own body where she was tense or holding back."[7] An intuitive awareness or rapport can develop during the course of labor to the point health professional and client seem to be communicating in a nonverbal language that probably has its roots in a combination of both subliminal and paranormal perceptions of the client's needs.

How do telesomatic symptoms differ from empathy? *A telesomatic symptom is a psi-mediated physiological response and a form of ESP. Empathy may be either a telesomatic symptom or the result of subliminally perceived impressions.*

It is not always possible to distinguish between a true telesomatic symptom—that is, a psi-mediated physiological response—and a subliminally perceived symptom, which triggers a psychosomatic reaction in the health professional. For example, Brian, a massage therapist, frequently feels the physical symptoms of others in his own body. "Sometimes a client will tell me what's wrong or what they think is wrong," says Brian. "Sometimes I'll make the observation myself by observing body position, mannerisms, limps, stretches, and so on, that cue me to a disorder. However, other times I feel the symptom.

"When I do feel it, it's usually when I'm doing a general bodyworking session, involving energy transfer in a quiet, relaxing atmosphere. Then I start feeling symptoms.

"What I feel most often is a headache or a stomachache or a physical pain in a certain area. Less often I'll pick up something like nausea, fever, or a tickling in the throat. It's a feeling where the headache or whatever doesn't feel like mine, so I do some checking to see if it belongs to the client.

"I don't try to feel them, but I'm relaxed and open, and it just hits me. I have little control over it, but when it happens, it's valid."

This may be the result of subliminally perceived perceptions of the other client's body movements and so on. However, when they wake a physician from a sound sleep, it is more likely ESP.

In either case, empathy can assist the health care provider to make a more accurate diagnosis, providing the health professional doesn't take on the physical symptoms to the point of becoming ill.

RESOLVING EMOTIONAL CONFLICTS

One in every four American mothers gives birth via cesarean surgery. There is no question: cesarean births are sometimes necessary. Cesareans have saved the lives of mother and/or baby. Unlike any other form of surgery, there is something special about a cesarean, a reason to celebrate. A child is born!

However, most health professionals agree that many if not most of these cesareans are unnecessary. Though some mothers seem to suffer no emotionally negative consequences from cesarean birth, others suffer long-term emotional scars. Although the birth of a child is a joyous event, the mother may feel cheated, deprived, even inadequate about not having given birth vaginally. The father may feel he is to blame.

Using relaxation and guided imagery methods (such as those in chapter 4) can assist the parents in letting go of the trauma the cesarean may have created.

There are two ways to do this:

- The mother can re-create the birth scene and imagine the outcome as she wishes it had occurred. This sometimes can bring powerful feelings to the surface, allowing the parents to grieve over the loss of the vaginal birth.
- The parents can use their intuition to mentally imagine each person at the birth scene and forgive that person if he or she may have been responsible for the cesarean. The parents must be sure to forgive themselves as well. Forgiveness is a powerful healing tool, clearing the way for the mother to give birth vaginally the next time around.

If you feel that you have yourself suffered traumatic births or intrauterine experiences, contact a psychotherapist or hypnotherapist who specializes in reliving birth memories (if you can locate such a person in your area). Transuterine communication may be a powerful method of resolving emotional conflicts in unwanted pregnancies. Health professionals have found that this method can help parents clarify their feelings and make a decision about whether to continue the pregnancy.

For example, before having an abortion, Stella, a woman who became unexpectedly pregnant, had a dream that she felt prepared her for the tragic event.

"I dreamed I was in communication with the fetus," Stella recalls. "In the dream, I explained to the baby that it really did not want to be born unwanted. I explained that I didn't want someone to grow up as an unwanted child because I had been one, and that seemed to me to be a very cruel thing.

"I also dreamed that the fetus was okay with this. I don't believe this was some sort of ESP but just my own unconscious process, helping me resolve my feelings."

Some mothers with unwanted pregnancies do consciously what Stella did in a dream. In fact, family counselor Barbara Findeisen pioneered an unusual method of helping mothers resolve their feelings before aborting unwanted pregnancies. She asked the mothers to talk to their unborn child before the procedure. This seemingly peculiar advice had a healing effect. Findeisen found that it eased the emotional trauma of abortion.

However, the method turned out to have an unexpected twist that surprised Findeisen. Talking with the soon-to-be aborted baby sometimes led to spontaneous miscarriage Soon after the mother told the baby her plans, the child, it seemed, left on its own.[8]

Hypnotherapist Helen Watkins also uses a method of transuterine communication with pregnant women who are trying to decide whether or not to terminate the pregnancy. She asks the mother to imagine the baby in any way that feels natural to her. The mother then speaks silently to her child expressing her conflict about the pregnancy. If she has decided to have the abortion, she explains, often in a tearful dialogue, why she cannot continue with the pregnancy. She then visualizes the baby leaving her body and may even ask the child to leave.

Helen Watkins finds this method healing. Transuterine communication, she feels, "opens the grieving process prior to the loss of the fetus."[9] She points out: "The client finds emotional release in this procedure, and with the emotional release comes a reduction of guilt."[10]

Like Barbara Findeisen's clients, women who consulted Helen Watkins sometimes miscarried just before the abortion date. For example, one pregnant woman, Mary, miscarried two days before her scheduled surgical appointment. Another mother miscarried the same day as her appointment.

Both women felt they had communicated with the baby. They felt the baby understood and agreed. "They reacted to these communications with a sense of awe," writes Helen Watkins, "respect of another energy system, and a sense of love by the fetus in agreeing to end its existence."[11]

Dr. Clara Riley also recommends communicating with the unborn child in cases of unwanted pregnancy. A client who was planning to terminate her pregnancy, had the following tearful dialogue with her unborn child: "I feel this isn't the right time for you be there, growing. . . . I couldn't give you what you want. The love wouldn't be there. The attention. Everything a baby needs. There would be tension and stress. You would be miserable.

"You should have warmth and love surrounded by happiness and I can't give that to you. I want you to go away. I ask you to go away.

"There's no other way. I don't want to have to do what I have to do tomorrow. Please go away on your own. Please hear me as I'm as close to you now as I'll ever be. And I'm sorry. I really am sorry."

The following day, the mother miscarried.[12]

HEALING

If a person can experience the symptoms of another, can he or she influence the symptoms of another with ESP?

Yes. Carefully controlled clinical studies have shown clearly the effects of "psychic" healing on induced wounds in mice.[13] Studies have even shown effects on the growth of barley seeds.[14]

Dr. Bernard Grad of McGill University worked with a man named Oskar Estabany who had psychic healing abilities. He placed surgically wounded mice into three groups. One group healed during the normal course of events without "psychic intervention." A person who did not have psychic healing abilities attempted to heal the second group. Mr. Estabany held cages of the third group twice daily for fifteen minutes. This group healed much more rapidly than the other two groups.

Dr. Grad arranged to have planted barley seeds divided into two groups. One group was watered with ordinary water. The other group received water "psychically charged" by being held in containers in Mr. Estabany's hands. The second group of barley plants grew more and slightly larger plants. To eliminate the possibility that Mr. Estabany might be somehow chemically treating the water to skew the results, the experiment was repeated with sealed beakers. The results were the same.

Though this is clearly a parapsychological phenomenon with tremendous implications in healing, there are no doubt physiological reasons why this mysterious process takes place. Sister Justa Smith, chairman of the chemistry department of Rosary Hill College Buffalo,

New York, was determined to find out why this worked. She hypothesized that healing was caused by the psychically affecting enzymatic activity in the body. Increased enzyme activity, in turn, augmented other chemical activity in the body, which led to more rapid healing. In one unusual experiment, she used four sealed bottles containing the enzyme trypsin. She subjected the first bottle to ultraviolet light, which decreases enzyme activity; the second bottle to a magnetic field, which increases enzyme activity; a third bottle to Mr. Estabany's hands; and a fourth bottle as a control (subjected to no intervention). Mysteriously, Mr. Estabany's psychic healing equalled the effect of the magnetic fields.[15]

HEALING EXERCISES

Here are two simple healing exercises based on beaming light to an injured area or person.

- Imagine that an aura of radiant light is surrounding and filling the area in need of healing. For example, if you've had a cesarean birth, imagine the incision site surrounded and bathed in radiant light. At the same time, picture the area as healed.
- To assist a baby or other person to heal, you can imagine that person surrounded by an aura of light. At the same time, send the person healing thoughts and emotions. Or feel yourself embracing the person with love. To try this exercise, you needn't be in the same room with the person.

Many health professionals use a similar exercise involving sending imaginary light to the person in need of healing. Not everyone has the same ability to heal. Just as a few people are especially gifted in telepathy, some have better success at ESP healing. However, it is certainly worth trying. If you'd like to attempt healing yourself or another, try the following exercise. Be sure you are also getting competent health care at the same time. Intuition is no substitute for medical care. If nothing else, this exercise may send a feeling of peace, comfort, and love via the extrasensory bond every parent and child shares.

CREATING AN EASIER, SAFER BIRTH

Gradually, as our society and our health care system becomes more *holistic*—embracing mind, body, and emotions rather than just physical symptoms—we are learning to pay greater attention to the mother's intuition. This is true whether health professionals want to call that intuition by the name ESP or simply a gut instinct.

However we name it, it is time that we turn inward to look for something that often proves safer than medical intervention and give ear to what may be the expectant mother's most valuable resource: her inner self.

CHAPTER 12

LOOKING AHEAD

Viva, a mother in Texas, remembers an incredible event that occurred when her little girl was ten years old. Sixty-four years later, the event still remains fresh in Viva's mind.

"My daughter had gone with my mother to Chicago to visit my sister," Viva recalls. "One day while she was gone I drove to Houston. As I was crossing a railroad, the arms that come down before a train passes came down on the top of my car. It was very frightening for I thought a train was coming and I couldn't move my car. In a little while, a crew of workmen came and got them off my car."

"Several days later, a letter came from my daughter. This is what she wrote: 'Dear Mother, Last night I had a terrible dream. I dreamed that you were crossing a railroad track and those things came down on your car. It scared me so that I woke up. Please write and tell me it was not true!' "

Similar numerous cases of ESP reported throughout the world may represent just the tip of the iceberg. Some form of ESP may be an integral part of the love bond we share with our children, a bond that unites parents and offspring at the deepest levels of the psyche. And our first taste of intuition may begin during the life-creating months of pregnancy, while the baby is tinier than a pinpoint.

Experiences such as Viva's are probably as old as human birth. Though few of us have such dramatic encounters with the world beyond the five senses, everyone probably has an unseen link with parent, child, family, and perhaps even all life. Everyone has intuitive ability.

Despite our culture's almost 100 percent reliance on logic, intuitive experiences have a way of breaking through to the surface now and then. This seems to be especially true during the life-creating months of pregnancy when mother, father, and child often discover intuition for the first time.

A LOST WAY OF KNOWING

As a society, however, we have lost touch with this most basic—and most mysterious—way of knowing. We have come to rely almost entirely on our logical, rational mind and shrug off intuition as valueless. Sadly, we have been taught—by the example of our culture—to ignore our intuition. Parapsychologists have observed that skepticism about intuition in our culture may contribute to its suppression. Study after study show that intuition is more common in children who have not yet been taught that this process is "abnormal."

Fear of ridicule can dampen intuitive ability or make one feel intuitive experiences are better off hidden. For example, Weston Agor, professor and director of the Master in Public Administration Program at the University of Texas at El Paso and author of *Intuition Management*, has found that many top executives whose major decisions are guided by intuition tend to keep it a secret.

One woman, a top-ranking corporate executive, admits: "At work, I work with men, men who tend to regard the use of intuition as suspect, female, and unscientific. . . . If I revealed my 'secret,' I'd have an ever harder time persuading them to accept my suggestions. They wouldn't regard my ideas or decisions as being properly rational. Yet they can justify the worst kind of screw-ups with a chart and a computer printout."[1]

A male manager admitted feeling a similar objection about expressing his intuition.

"I have tried explanations without success. Also, superiors seem to believe some sort of witchcraft or other dark art is being employed. Better to use it to advantage than go through the hassle of explanation. I've even gotten to the point of telling others I'm just a good guesser."[2]

Another top executive at one of America's most successful corporations put it this way: "Sometimes one must dress up a gut decision in 'data clothes' to make it more acceptable or palatable, but this fine tuning is usually after the fact of the decision."[3]

Because of negative attitudes about intuition, some parents are reluctant to relate their intuitive experiences to their health care providers.

They fear having their intuition belittled and dismissed as unimportant. It is time we reversed this trend and valued our inner voice.

THE REBIRTH OF INTUITION

This may be just what our culture is beginning to do. Many are learning to pay attention to inner feelings, intuition. As a result, intuition is gradually gaining acceptance in contemporary society. Allowing intuition to influence our lives means more than just adopting a new way of knowing. It spells a transformation of our values and belief systems. A wide variety of lay people and professionals alike, including environmentalists, holistic health care practitioners, and childbirth professionals, are working toward this goal.

Business consultant Henry Mintzberg emphasizes the value of heeding intuition. Decision making under pressure, he points out in a *Harvard Business Review* article, belongs to the realm of intuition.[4] He advises combining the right hemisphere world of intuition with the left hemisphere of rational thinking and logic for maximum results.

In science, in new discoveries, intuition is often the vanguard of world-transforming breakthroughs. Both Jonas Salk, creator of the Salk vaccine for polio, and Buckminster Fuller, world-renowned engineer, attribute their discoveries largely to intuition.[5]

The same applies to the childbearing professions. Inspiration from intuition combined with reasoning and experience can enhance clinical skills from diagnosis to providing more well-rounded maternity care.

But will the mystery ever be dispelled? Or will we just expand our awareness to the point where we are more comfortable with phenomena that are beyond the personal self?

Psychologist Lawrence LeShan, Ph.D., who has done breakthrough research in healing, writes: "Behind all the paranormal and the mystical lies the knowledge of the essential unity of many, with his fellows and the rest of the cosmos."[6]

And at no time is this more true than during participation in the childbearing miracle. For many parents, coming to terms with the creative energy of birth, turning inward and trusting the mother's own body to create new life as nature designed, is a life-transforming event that goes hand in hand with unlocking a new way of perceiving the world.

As one new mother put it: "I never felt closer to the heart of creation than I did while giving birth. Sure it hurt, but I was more confident, more alive than I've ever felt!"

RITE OF PASSAGE

Perhaps one of the most valuable gifts that greater respect for intuition will offer our society is a more holistic maternity care system based on meeting the mother's intuitively felt needs. We've already discussed how laboring women who heed their intuition tend to know just what position to adopt and just what to do to best benefit their baby. And we've seen how opening up to intuition can assist the health professional to provide better maternity care. Now let's look at how intuition can affect the future of childbirth practices in a more universal way than just the birth of one child or the practice of one health care provider.

Throughout the world, many cultures have developed a system of ritual—a patterned, repetitive, symbolic act with cultural, magical, or religious significance—to cope with the raw, primitive power of birth and even to hide themselves from the fear of it.

For millennia, childbirth has been associated with rituals. In that magnificent collection of folklore, *The Golden Bough,* Sir James Frazer records numerous incidents of knot tying or untying rituals common throughout he world.[7] For example, the Saxons of Transylvania believe that the birth process will be easier if the all the knots in a mother's garments are untied. They also unlock all the doors and boxes in the house. The Lapps also feel that laboring mothers should not have knots in their garments. Similarly, in ancient India, all the knots were untied during childbirth.

Those who attended the rites of Juno Lucina, the goddess of childbirth, in ancient Rome, were required to wear garments without knots.

A similar idea no doubt underlies opening doors and locks, another custom practiced throughout the civilized and primitive worlds alike. On the island of Calsette, near Bombay, all doors and drawers are unlocked with a key when a mother is having a difficult labor.

Knot untying rituals are not limited to women. Just as men participate in pregnancy even to the point of sometimes experiencing prenatal symptoms, expectant fathers take part in the rites of pregnancy in many cultures throughout the world. Among the Toumbuluh tribe of North Celebes, the expectant father is not permitted to sit with his legs crossed or to tie tight knots.[8] The Mandelings of Sumatra carry the door-opening custom to an extreme. They not only open the lids of chests and boxes when the mother is having a difficult labor, but the father "has to strike the projecting ends of some of the house beams in order to loosen them."[9]

Door-opening and knot-untying customs may symbolize the mother's intuitive knowledge that, in order to give birth most easily, she needs to symbolically "uncross her legs," open and surrender to the life-creating power of labor, a power greater than herself. Some mothers find wearing their own garment (associated with health and feeling normal) rather than a hospital gown (associated with illness) helps them open more easily. Wearing one's own gown may be a modern form of knot untying to combat the negative effect of laboring in a highly clinical setting.

The clinical setting may sometimes be necessary. However, childbirth rituals that prevailed into the early 1990s of our modern society may be detrimental. In fact, if centuries from today anthropologists were to take a look at some of the birth customs in vogue only a few years ago, they would probably think they were seeing more ritual than science. Some of these birth rituals, in contrast to those of ancient society, such as the rite of untying knots, tend to bind rather than release the mother.

Psychiatrist Thomas Verny, former president of the Pre- and Perinatal Psychology Association of North America, says: "Many hi-tech tests, procedures, and routines used in obstetrics have no proven efficacy and are really more in the nature of rituals than medical interventions. What is held to be scientific is often just the ritualization of an unproven belief."[10]

This doesn't mean technology doesn't have a place in birth. Nor does it devalue the role of appropriate medical intervention. However, it should give us pause to think that we may be overusing technology. According to pediatrician and epidemiologist Marsden G. Wagner of the World Health Organization, "Obstetrical intervention rates in the United States far exceed those of any country in Europe. Indeed, the cesarean section rate in the United States ranges from nearly double to over triple that of the European countries . . . countries with some of the lowest perinatal mortality rates in the world have cesarean section rates of less than 10 percent."[11]

Our national cesarean rate, one of the highest in the world, has soared from 4 percent in 1970 to greater than 25 percent—meaning one in every four American mothers gives birth via major abdominal surgery. Yet this dramatic rise in cesareans has produced no subsequent improvement in infant or maternal mortality rates.[12]

Texas anthropology professor, Robbie Davis-Floyd, Ph.D., investigated obstetrical procedures from an anthropological perspective. After an extensive examination of OB routines, she concluded that many technological interventions could be ritual gestures. Throughout history birth rituals give control over what may be beyond control and to hide dangers perceived to be present in the passage rite.[13] Modern birth rituals, Dr. Davis-Floyd feels, may be a "rational ritual response to our technological society's extreme fear of the natural processes on which it still depends for its continued existence."[14]

"Everything possible is done to desexualize what is naturally a sexual event," continues Dr. Davis-Floyd, "because sex is a very powerful natural process and the true creator of new life and perpetuator of culture."[15]

"Many medical procedures replace religious ones," she writes, fulfilling many of the same purposes and satisfying many of the same cultural and psychological needs. Moreover, while most cultures seem content to use their baptismal rituals to make the baby 'human,' we in our arrogance use our entire set of birth rituals to actually make it appear that our babies are cultural products."[16]

For example, Dr. Davis considers the *episiotomy,* a surgical incision performed to widen the birth outlet, a ritual gesture without medical value. In rare cases an episiotomy is useful. For example, if the baby is severely distressed and a short birth is essential or the shoulders are "stuck" in the birth outlet (a conditon called "shoulder dystocia"), an episiotomy is warranted. For the majority, however, the episiotomy can almost always be avoided. An extensive search of the medical literature reveals no support for the routine episiotomies performed by the majority of U.S. obstetricians."[17]

Obstetricians are quick to point out that a neat incision is easier to repair than a ragged tear. But this overlooks an obvious fact: no tear requires no repair.

In the Netherlands, a country with much less focus on obstetrical intervention than the United States, almost all health practitioners consider the episiotomy unnecessary. The Dutch episiotomy rate is 6 percent compared to close to 90 percent in the United States.

A few American physicians and many midwives use perineal massage (gentle message of the tissues in the area of the birth outlet, especially between vagina and anus) and hot compresses to help the laboring woman avoid tearing. More important, they have learned to trust the mother's body to give birth without unnecessary surgery.

An even more bizarre ritual is shaving the pubic hair—a custom performed in many hospitals even in the 1990s. This odd custom is now thankfully falling by the wayside and no longer performed in all but a few hospitals. The medical reason behind the pubic shave? To prevent infection. The fact is, it increases infection.[18]

The use of a hospital bed for normal labor may yet be another ritual that is not only uncomfortable but has no useful value for the mother. In fact, being put to bed gives the laboring woman the impression that she is sick, a patient, rather than a participant in a normal life process. Perceiving herself as sick, in turn, alienates her from her own inner strength and her intuition. Her power is limited, and she is brought under control of the cultural system.

BALANCING INTUITION WITH TECHNOLOGY

Encouraged to follow her intuitive voice, few women would take to bed during labor. Research has repeatedly shown that the upright position hastens labor's progress and is more comfortable for most women.[19] Perhaps the cruelest and most bizarre American birth ritual is separating mother and infant immediately after birth. The routine use of the central nursery is a custom as weird as anything recorded in anthropological literature in the history of mankind.

Until just a few years ago, the baby was whisked away from mother immediately after birth and placed into a central nursery, which one obstetrician described as a "concentration camp" for newborns. In pain, babies screamed for mother. In pain, mothers cried for baby. In most hospitals, mother-infant separation is now reserved for medical emergencies.

Animal breeders wouldn't think of handling a birth in such a manner—because they realize separating mother and offspring could have long-term detrimental effects on both. If animal mothers are separated from their young for as short a time as one to four hours during this sensitive period, the mother often fails to provide for her young.

Can we delude ourselves into believing that humans are less sensitive than animals?

Maternal-infant separation during the first hours after birth may be the prime contributing factor toward the development of baby blues— a constellation of tears, irritability, and depression that afflicts some 80 percent of U.S. mothers beginning the third to fifth day after giving birth. The baby blues are so common that most people believe they are a natural consequence of giving birth and the result of hormonal changes. However, according to Helen Varney of the Maternal-Newborn Program at Yale University's School of Nursing, "Postpartum blues are largely a psychological phenomenon of the woman who is separated from her family and her baby."[20]

Thanks to paying attention to new mothers' instincts, most health care providers no longer separate mothers from babies except in case of medical emergencies. The results have shown dramatic improvements in newborns. A study conducted at Duke University in North Carolina showed that the breast-feeding rate increased more than 50 percent when mothers had no option but to room with their infants.[21] Infants who remain with the mother immediately after birth tend to have fewer infections for the first year, gain more weight, and are breast-fed longer.[22]

Because greater attention is given to women's intuition in incorporating such professionals as childbirth companions during birth, we are rethinking the way we approach childbirth. Our culture is in the process of emerging from an obstetrical dark age. Until recently, contemporary society had all but lost touch with the natural miracle of labor and birth. Modern science and medicine made pregnancy a thing to be measured, quantified, and monitored. In conventional hospitals, childbirth was often approached as if it were a medical event, a procedure like an appendectomy. And medicine substituted meeting the mother's and baby's emotional needs with technical intervention.

Healthy, rewarding options for mother and baby are today replacing the dehumanizing maternity care of the past. Whether in hospital, childbearing center, or at home, our culture is beginning to discover there is more to creating life than we can measure on a monitor screen or quantify in a laboratory. The newborn's cry, the elation and joy in the parents' eyes, the love bond that unites parent and child will always remain beyond the realm of medicine. For the health care professional who puts parents and child before procedure, being with a laboring woman can be a humbling and learning experience.

SUMMING UP

Sir James Frazer tells of an ancient Roman custom involving presenting the mother with a key as a symbol of an easier birth. We, too, can present the mother with a key to an easier childbirth in modern society.

Repeated parapsychological research has shown that the attitude of the experimenter somehow influences the results of the experiment—appropriately called the "experimenter effect." A similar phenomenon occurs during labor, wherein the attitudes of the staff person markedly affect the mother's experience of labor. Some professionals have an "opening presence."

Creating an opening presence, that is, a manner conducive to helping the mother surrender to labor, may be simply a matter of recognizing the importance of the parents' intuition. Allowing the mother to do what she feels intuitively, whether she gives birth in the hospital, childbearing center, or home, may have a profound impact on her labor. Combining intuition with appropriate medical supervision can help women to labor more easily.

Paying greater attention to the mother's intuitively felt needs during birth may have lifelong consequences on her family.

We've heard from some of the children who have had traumatic births. Let's now hear from some of the children who remember being born into loving arms—the way mothers' intuition would have it.

Elaine, a girl under hypnosis, recalls distinctly her first look at her mother: "She is sitting up in bed ready to breast-feed me. She looks tired but happy. I had a blanket, a pink blanket, and I'm trying to look out and see what she looks like. . . . She has her arms out and she's smiling. The nurse is gently handing me to her; I appreciate the gentleness. My mother cradles me in her left arm and she keeps looking at me and I keep looking at her. I feel like I will reach up and grab her finger. . . . I feel like there is someone who understands that I have needs right now. And I don't want a lot of attention for screaming. I want to get attention by cooing and making her smile. So I try to do those kinds of things and she responds like crazy. . . . I'm glad for the time with my mom."[23]

And Marianne relives what it was like to be welcomed by dad: "My dad is holding me; that feels really good. He likes me. I feel really happy. He said I'm his little girl. This makes me feel good. In my dad's arms it's almost as good as being inside mother."[24]

Isn't it time we paid attention to what our children have to teach us? Perhaps they can teach us to reconnect to our intuitive, inner nature: the special way of knowing. The first step in doing this may be turning to the womb. The place where it all begins.

NOTES

CHAPTER 1: A CASE OF THE INEXPLICABLE

1. A. Feldmar, "The Embryology of Consciousness: What Is a Normal Pregnancy?" in *The Psychological Aspects of Abortion*, D. Mall and W. Watts, eds., (Washington, D.C.: University Publications of America, 1979), pp. 15–24.

2. A. Mills, "A Preliminary Investigation of Cases of Reincarnation Among the Beaver and Gitskan Indians," *Anthropologica* XXX (1988) p. 52.

CHAPTER 2: DO EXPECTANT MOTHERS HAVE ESP?

1. L. Sprecher, cited in Weston Agor, "The Logic of Intuition: How Top Executives Make Important Decisions," *Organizational Dynamics* (1986): p. 6.

2. I. Stevenson, *Telepathic Impressions: A Review and Report of Thirty-Five New Cases* (Charlottesville: University Press of Virginia, 1970) p. 15.

3. J. Prasad, and I. Stevenson, "A Survey of Spontaneous Psychical Experiences in School Children of Uttar Pradesh, India," *International Journal of Parapsychology*, 10 (1968) pp. 241–61.

4. C. Backster, "Evidence of Primary Perception in Plant Life," *International Journal of Parapsychology*, 10:4 (1968).

5. D. S. Rogo, *Parapsychology: A Century of Inquiry* (New York: Taplinger, 1973), pp. 86–87.

6. G. H. Estabrooks, *Bulletin, Boston Society for Psychical Research*, 5 (1927), cited in D. S. Rogo, *Parapsychology: A Century of Inquiry* (New York: Taplinger, 1973), p. 74.

7. C. G. Jung, *Psychology and Religion: West and East* (New York: Pantheon, 1958), p. 592.

8. J. Ehrenwald, *The ESP Experience: A Psychiatric Validation* (New York: Basic Books, 1978), p. 13.

9. F. Vaughan, *Awakening Intuition* (New York: Doubleday, 1979), p. 48, 66, 69.

10. Weston Agor, "The Logic of Intuition: How Top Executives Make Important Decisions," *Organizational Dynamics* (1986): p. 10.

11. C. Tart, "The Physical Universe, the Spiritual Universe, and the Paranormal," *Transpersonal Psychologies* (New York: Harper and Row, 1975), pp. 132–33.

12. D. S. Rogo, *Parapsychology: A Century of Inquiry* (New York: Taplinger, 1973), p. 111.

13. I. Stevenson, "Cultural Patterns in Cases Suggestive of Reincarnation Among the Tlingit Indians of Southeastern Alaska," *Journal of the American Society for Psychical Research* 60:2 (1966): p. 240.

14. Weston, Agor "The Logic of Intuition: How Top Executives Make Important Decisions," *Organizational Dynamics* (1986): p. 10.

CHAPTER 3: THE METAMORPHOSIS OF PREGNANCY

1. J. Ehrenwald, *The ESP Experience: A Psychiatric Validation* (New York: Basic Books, 1978), p. 21.

2. Ibid.

3. Ibid.

4. Ibid., p. 24.

5. L. Salk, "The Role of the Heartbeat in the Relations Between Mother and Infant," *Scientific American* (May 1973): p. 29.

6. D. B. Cheek, "Feto-Maternal Telepathic Communication and Its Significance," *Hypnos* 17:2 (1990): p. 77.

7. D. B. Cheek, "Are Telepathy, Clairvoyance and 'Hearing' Possible in Utero? Suggestive Evidence as Revealed During Hypnotic Age-Regression Studies in Prenatal Memory," *Pre- and Perinatal Psychology Journal* 7:2 (Winter 1992): pp. 125–37.

8. E. Gurney, F. Myers, and F. Podmore, *Phantasms of the Living,* (New York: Arno Press, 1975), pp. 137–38.

9. H. Parad, and S. Caplan, "A Framework for Studying in Crisis" from *Crisis Intervention: Selected Readings* (New York: Family Services Association of America, 1969) cited in Laurie Sherwen, *Psychosocial Dimensions of the Pregnant Family* (New York: Springer Publishing, 1987), pp. 20–21.

10. Laurie Sherwen, *Psychosocial Dimensions of the Pregnant Family* (New York: Springer Publishing, 1987), pp. 20–21.

11. P. Maybruck, *Pregnancy and Dreams* (Los Angeles: Jeremy Tarcher, 1989), p. 11.

12. I. Stevenson, *Telepathic Impressions: A Review and Report of Thirty-Five New Cases,* (Charlottesville: University Press of Virginia, 1970): p. 16.

13. J. Ehrenwald, "Right vs. Left-Hemispheric Approach in Psychical Research," *Journal of the American Society for Psychical Research* 78 (1984): p. 29.

14. Ibid., p. 33.

15. P. Maybruck, *Pregnancy and Dreams* (Los Angeles: Jeremy Tarcher, 1989), p. 49.

16. G. Peterson, and L. Mehl, *Pregnancy as Healing: A Holistic Philosophy for Prenatal Care,* 2 vols. (Berkeley: Mind/Body Press.)

17 E. Neumann, *The Great Mother* (Princeton, N.J.: Princeton University Press, 1974), p. 96.

18. Ibid.

19. Leni Schwartz, *Bonding Before Birth* (Boston: Sigo Press, 1991), p. 64.

20. Ibid., p. 48.

CHAPTER 4: COUVADE SYNDROME

1. Helen Diner, cited in D. Meltzer, *BIRTH: An Anthology of Ancient Texts, Songs, Prayers, and Stories* (San Francisco: North Point Press, 1981), p. 87.

2. O. S. Davis., "Mood and Symptoms of Expectant Fathers During the Course of Pregnancy: A Study of the Crisis Perspective of Expectant Fatherhood, Doctoral Dissertation (University of North Carolina, Greensboro, 1977), *Dissertation Abstracts International* 38: 5841A.

3. K. E. Reid, "Fatherhood and Emotional Stress: The Couvade Syndrome," *Journal of Social Welfare* 2:1 (1975): 13–14.

4. B. Malinowski, *Sex and Repression in Savage Society* (London: Kegan Paul, 1937), p. 285.

5. W. H. Trethowan and M. F. Conlon, "The Couvade Syndrome," *British Journal of Psychiatry* 111 (1965): 59.

6. Ibid., p. 57.

7. M. D. Jensen, R. Benson, and I. Boback, *Maternity Care: The Nurse and the Family* (St. Louis: Mosby, 1981), p. 289.

8. J. F. Clinton, "Expectant Fathers at Risk for Couvade," *Nursing Research* 35:5 (1986): 290–95.

9. Ibid., p. 290.

10. M. Lipkin, G. Lamb, G. "The Couvade Syndrome: An Epidemiologic Study," *Annals of Internal Medicine* 96:4 (1982): 511.

11. J. F. Clinton, "Expectant Fathers at Risk for Couvade," *Nursing Research* 35:5 (1986): 294.

12. J. F. Clinton, "Couvade: Patterns, Predictors, and Nursing Management: A Research Proposal Submitted to the Division of Nursing," *Western Journal of Nursing Research* 7:2 (1985): 233.

13. W. H. Trethowan and M. F. Conlon, "The Couvade Syndrome," *British Journal of Psychiatry* 111 (1965): 58–59.

14. I. Stevenson, *Telepathic Impressions: A Review and Report of Thirty-Five New Cases* (Charlottesville: University Press of Virginia, 1970), pp. 117–124.

15. R. Heywood, "Case of Rapport between Mother and Daughter," *Journal of the Society of Psychical Research* 42 (1963): 187–189.

16. B. E. Schwarz, *Psychic Nexus: Psychic Phenomena in Psychiatry and Everyday Life* (New York: Van Nostrand Rheinhold, 1980), p. 117.

17. I. Stevenson, *Telepathic Impressions: A Review and Report of Thirty-Five New Cases* (Charlottesville: University Press of Virginia, 1970), p. 109.

18. C. Jung, *Memories, Dreams, Reflections* (New York: Pantheon, 1963), p. 38.

19. L. E. Rhine, *Foundation for Research on the Nature of Man Bulletin* 1:2 (1965): 4.

20. E. D. Dean, "Plethysmograph Results Over Distances and Through a Screen," *Journal of Parapsychology* 28 (1964): 285.

21. C. Tart, "The Physical Universe, the Spiritual Universe, and the Paranormal," *Transpersonal Psychologies* (New York: Harper and Row, 1975), p. 134.

CHAPTER 5: THOUGHTS: MUSIC OF THE UNBORN

1. D. B. Chamberlain, "Is There Intelligence Before Birth?" *Pre- and Perinatal Psychology Journal* 6:3 (1992): 223.

2. A. W. Liley, "The Foetus as a Personality," *Pre- and Perinatal Psychology* 5:3 (1991): 192–93.

3. J. C. Birnholz, "The Development of Human Fetal Eye Movement Patterns," *Science* 213 (1981): 679–681.

4. M. Murooka, Y. Koie, and N. Suda, "Analysis of Intra-uterine Sounds and their Soothing Effect on the Newly-Born," *Journal of Gynecology and Obstetrics* (1976): 367–376.

5. A. W. Liley, "The Foetus as a Personality," *Pre- and Perinatal Psychology Journal* 5:3 (1991): 200.

6. H. Weiland, "Heartbeat Rhythm and Maternal Behavior," *Journal of Child Psychiatry* 3 (1964): 161–164.

7. L. Salk, "The Role of the Heartbeat in the Relations Between Mother and Infant," *Scientific American* (May 1973): 24–29.

8. Ethan Zimmer and Michael Divon, "Fetal Vibroaccoustic Stimulation," *Journal of Obstetrics and Gynecology* 81:3 (March 1993): 451; Ethan Zimmer, et al., "Vibroaccoustic Stimulation Evokes Human Fetal Micturition," *Journal of Obstetrics and Gynecology* (February 1993): 565.

9. P. G. Hepper, "Fetal 'Soap' Addiction," *Lancet* (June 1988): 1347–1348.

10. Roberta K. Panneton, "Prenatal Auditory Experience With Melodies: Effects on Post-natal Auditory Preferences in Human Newborns," Ph.D. Dissertation, University of North Carolina, Greensboro, *Dissertation Abstracts* 47:9 (March 1987):

11. R. E. Laibow, "Birth Recall: A Clinical Report," *Pre- and Perinatal Psychology Journal* 1:1 (1986): 78–81.

12. C. Olds, "A Sound Start in Life," *Pre- and Perinatal Psychology Journal* 1:1 (1986): 82–85 [R].

13. David Chamberlain, *Babies Remember Birth* (Los Angeles: Jeremy Tarcher, 1988), p. 23.

14. Y. Ando and H. Hattori, "Effects of Intense Noise During Fetal Life Upon Postnatal Adaptability," *Journal of Acoustical Society of America* 47 (1970): 1128–1130.

15. Y. Ando and H. Hattori, "Effects of Noise on Human Placental Lactogen (HPL) Levels in Maternal Plasma," *British Journal of Obstetrics and Gynecology* 84 (1977): 115–118.

16. H. M. Truby, "Prenatal and Neonatal Speech" in *Child Language,* a special issue of *WORD* 27, parts, 1–3 (1975): 67.

17. A. DeCasper and W. Fifer "Of Human Bonding: Newborns Prefer Their Mother's Voices," *Science* 208 (1980): 1174–1176.

18. A. DeCasper and M. Spence, "Prenatal Maternal Speech Influences Human Newborn Auditory Preferences," Paper presented at the Third Biennial International Conference on Infant Studies, Austin, Texas, 1982, cited in David Chamberlain, "Prenatal Intelligence," Chapter one in Thomas Blum, ed., *Prenatal Perception, Learning and Bonding* (Seattle: Leonardo Publishers, 1993).

19. David Chamberlain, "Prenatal Intelligence," Chapter one in Thomas Blum, ed., *Prenatal Perception, Learning and Bonding* (Seattle: Leonardo Publishers, 1993), p. 65.

20. Michael Lieberman, cited in L.W. Sontag, "Parental Determinants of Postnatal Behavior" in Harry Weisman and George Kerr, *Fetal Growth and Development* (New York: McGraw-Hill, 1970), p. 263.

21. H. E. Fox, et al., "Maternal Ethanol Ingestion and the Occurrence of Human Fetal Breathing Movements," *British Journal of Obstetrics and Gynecology* 132 (1978): 354–358.

22. G. Gennser, et al., "The Influence of External Factors on Breathing Movements in the Human Fetus," in G. Rooth and L. E. Bratteby, eds., *Perinatal Medicine* (Sweden: Almquist and Wiksell, 1976), pp. 181–86.

23. F. Manning, et al., "Effect of Cigarette Smoking on Fetal breathing Movements in Normal Pregnancies," *British Medical Journal* 1 (1975): 552; F. Manning and C. Feyerbead, "Cigarette Smoking and Fetal Breathing Movements," *British Journal of Obstetrics and Gynecology*, 83 (1976): 262.

24. Michael Lieberman, cited in L. W. Sontag, "Prenatal Determinants of Postnatal Behavior" in Harry Weisman and George Kerr, *Fetal Growth and Development* (New York: McGraw-Hill, 1970), p. 265.

25. N. Rossi, et al., "Maternal Stress and Fetal Motor Behavior: A Preliminary Report," *Pre- and Perinatal Psychology Journal* 3:4 (1989): 311–18.

26. Michael Lieberman, cited in L. W. Sontag, "Prenatal Determinants of Postnatal Behavior" in Harry Weisman and George Kerr, *Fetal Growth and Development* (New York: McGraw-Hill, 1970), p. 267.

27. B. H. Zuckerman, et al., "Maternal Depressive Symptoms during Pregnancy, and Newborn Irritability," *Developmental and Behavioral Pediatrics* 11:4 (1990): 190–94.

28. Ibid., p. 194.

29. D. B. Cheek, "Feto-Maternal Telepathic Communication and Its Significance," *Hypnos* 17:2 (1990): 72.

30. O. Rank, *The Trauma of Birth* (New York: Robert Brunner, 1952), p. 163.

31. David Chamberlain, *Babies Remember Birth* (Los Angeles: Jeremy Tarcher, 1988), p. xxi.

32. Ibid., p. 103.

33. Ibid., p. 99.

34. D. B. Chamberlain, "The Outer Limits of Memory," *Noetic Sciences Review* (Autumn 1990): 4–13.

35. D. B. Chamberlain, "The Significance of Birth Memories," *Pre- and Perinatal Psychology Journal* 2:4 (1988): 212.

36. D. B. Cheek, "Are Telepathy, Clairvoyance and 'Hearing' Possible in Utero? Suggestive Evidence as Revealed During Hypnotic Age-Regression Studies in Prenatal Memory," *Pre- and Perinatal Psychology Journal* 7:2 (Winter 1992): 127–128.

37. Ibid., pp. 131–34.

38. D. B. Cheek, "Prenatal and Perinatal Imprints: Apparent Prenatal Consciousness as Revealed by Hypnosis," *Pre- and Perinatal Psychology Journal* 1:2 (1986): 98.

39. V. L. Raikov, "Age Regression in Infancy by Adult Subjects in Deep Hypnosis," *American Journal of Clinical Hypnosis* 22:3 (1980): 156–63.

40. D. B. Chamberlain, "The Expanding Boundaries of Memory," *Pre- and Perinatal Psychology Journal* 4:3 (1990): 179.

41. D. B. Chamberlain, "The Outer Limits of Memory," *Noetic Sciences Review* (Autumn 1990): 4–13.

42. Ibid.

43. A. Feldmar, "The Embryology of Consciousness: What is a Normal Pregnancy?" in D. Mall and W. Watts, eds., *The Psychological Aspects of Abortion* (Washington, D. C.: University Publications of America, 1979), pp. 15–24.

44. D. B. Cheek, "Are Telepathy, Clairvoyance and 'Hearing' Possible in Utero? Suggestive Evidence as Revealed During Hypnotic Age-Regression Studies in Prenatal Memory," *Pre- and Perinatal Psychology Journal* 7:2 (Winter 1992): 128–131.

45. G. Farrant "Cellular Consciousness," *Aesthema, Journal of the International Primal Association* 7: (1986): 28–39.

46. J. E. Van Husen, "The Development of Fears, Phobias, and Restrictive Patterns of Adaptation Following Attempted Abortions," *Pre- and Perinatal Psychology Journal* 2:3 (1988): 179–85.

47. Ibid., p. 185.

48. A. Feldmar, "The Embryology of Consciousness: What Is a Normal Pregnancy?" in D. Mall and W. Watts, eds., *The Psychological Aspects of Abortion* (Washington, D. C.: University Publications of America, 1979), pp. 15–24.

49. D. B. Chamberlain, "The Outer Limits of Memory," *Noetic Sciences Review* (Autumn 1990): 4–13.

50. Ibid., pp. 4–13.

51. M. Sabom, *Recollections of Death: A Medical Investigation* (New York: Simon and Schuster, 1982).

52. R. Moody, *The Light Beyond* (New York: Bantam, 1988): pp. 134–45.

53. D. B. Chamberlain, "The Outer Limits of Memory," *Noetic Sciences Review* (Autumn 1990): 4–13.

54. D. B. Chamberlain, "The Expanding Boundaries of Memory," *Pre- and Perinatal Psychology Journal* 4:3 (1990): 173.

55. R. Sheldrake, "Can Our Memories Survive the Death of Our Brains?" in J. Spong, ed., *Proceedings on Consciousness and Survival*, Institute of Noetic Sciences, pp. 67–77.

56. C. Pert, "Neuropeptides, the Emotions and Bodymind," in J. Spong, ed., *Proceedings of the Symposium on Consciousness and Survival* (Sausalito, Calif: Institute of Noetic Sciences, 1987), pp. 79–89.

57. D. B. Chamberlain, "The Expanding Boundaries of Memory," *Pre- and Perinatal Psychology Journal* 4:3 (1990): 183.

CHAPTER 6: COMMUNICATING WITH YOUR UNBORN CHILD

1. D. B. Chamberlain, "The Expanding Boundaries of Memory," *Pre- and Perinatal Psychology Journal* 4:3 (1990): 185.

2. Cited in Leni Schwartz, *Bonding Before Birth* (Boston: Sigo Press, 1991), pp. 59–60.

3. R. F. Van de Carr and M. Lehrer, "Prenatal University; Commitment to Fetal-Family Bonding and the Strengthening of the Family Unit as an Educational Institution" *Pre- and Perinatal Psychology Journal* 3:2 (1988): 95.

4. M. Freeman, "Is Infant Learning Egocentric or Duocentric?" *Pre- and Perinatal Psychology Journal* 2:1 (1987): 25–42.

5. Ibid., p. 29.

6. R. F. Van de Carr and M. Lehrer, "Prenatal University; Commitment to Fetal-Family Bonding and the Strengthening of the Family Unit as an Educational Institution," *Pre- and Perinatal Psychology Journal* 3:2 (1988): 88.

7. Ibid.

8. Ibid., pp. 87–102.

9. Ibid., p. 95.

10. Mike Samuels and Nancy Samuels, *The Well Baby Book* (New York: Summit Books, 1979), p. 15.

11. Ibid., p. 36.

12. David Chamberlain, *Babies Remember Birth* (Los Angeles: Jeremy Tarcher, 1988), p. xxii.

CHAPTER 7: EXPECTANT PARENTS' DREAMS: DOORWAY
TO THE EXTRAORDINARY

1. R. Lederman, *Psychosocial Adaptation in Pregnancy* (Englewood Cliffs, N. J.: Prentice Hall, 1984).

2. A. Colman and L. Colman, *Earth Father, Sky Father: The Changing Concept of Fathering* (Englewood Cliffs, N.J.: Prentice Hall, 1981), p. 131.

3. C. Jung, *Man and His Symbols* (New York: Doubleday, 1964).

4. P. Maybruck, *Pregnancy and Dreams* (Los Angeles: Jeremy Tarcher, 1989), pp. 84–86.

5. Alan Siegel, *Pregnant Dreams: Developmental Process in the Manifest Dreams of Expectant Fathers*, Dissertation Abstract, unpublished copy, 1982, pp. 66–67.

6. Ibid., p. 121.

7. Ibid., p. 105.

8. P. Maybruck, *Pregnancy and Dreams* (Los Angeles: Jeremy Tarcher, 1989), p. 87.

9. Ibid., p. 39.

10 Ibid., pp. 27–28.

11. Ibid., p. 28.

12. Ibid., p. 29.

13. Ibid., p. 31.

14. Ibid., p. 34.

15. Leni Schwartz, *Bonding Before Birth* (Boston: Sigo Press, 1991), p. 231.

16. Alan Siegel, *Pregnant Dreams: Developmental Process in the Manifest Dreams of Expectant Fathers*, Dissertation Abstract, unpublished copy, 1982, p. 103.

17. I. Stevenson, "Cultural Patterns in Cases Suggestive of Reincarnation Among the Tlingit Indians of Southeastern Alaska," *Journal of the American Society for Psychical Research* 60:2 (1966): 237.

18. I. Stevenson, *Cases of the Reincarnation Type*, Vol. I: *Ten Cases in India* (Charlottesville, Virginia: University of Virginia Press, 1975): 68.

19. I. Wilson, *Reincarnation: The Claims Investigated* (New York: Penguin Books, 1982), p. 233.

20. I. Stevenson, "Cultural Patterns in Cases Suggestive of Reincarnation Among the Tlingit Indians of Southeastern Alaska," *Journal of the American Society for Psychical Research* 60:2 (1966): 239.

21. A. Mills, "A Preliminary Investigation of Cases of Reincarnation Among the Beaver and Gitskan Indians," *Anthropologica* 30 (1988): 37.

22. I. Stevenson, "Cultural Patterns in Cases Suggestive of Reincarnation Among the Tlingit Indians of Southeastern Alaska," *Journal of the American Society for Psychical Research* 60:2 (1966): 236.

23. Ibid., p. 229.

24. M. Ullman, S. Krippner, and A. Vaughan, *Dream Telepathy* (New York: Macmillan, 1973), p. 19.

25. C. Panthuraamphorn, "Prenatal Infant Stimulation Program in Thailand," Unpublished Study.

26. P. Maybruck, *Pregnancy and Dreams* (Los Angeles: Jeremy Tarcher, 1989), pp. 10–11.

27. Ibid., p. 153.

28. Ibid., p. 154.

29. S. Laberge, *Lucid Dreaming* (Los Angeles: Jeremy Tarcher, 1985), pp. 155–157.

30. P. Maybruck, *Pregnancy and Dreams* (Los Angeles: Jeremy Tarcher, 1989), p. 163.

31. Ibid., pp. 164–65.

CHAPTER 8: NESTING

1. Sir William Liley, "The Foetus as a Personality," *Australian and New Zealand Journal of Psychiatry* 6:2 (1972): 99–105.

2. Ibid., pp. 192–93.

3. D. B. Cheek, "Some Newer Understandings of Dreams in Relation to Threatened Abortion and Premature Labor," *Pacific Medicine and Surgery* 73 (1965): 379–84.

4. Ibid., p. 384.

5. Ibid.

6. Ibid., pp. 379–84.

7. Ibid.

8. D. Cheek, Personal communication, 1993.

9. D. B. Cheek, "Some Newer Understandings of Dreams in Relation to Threatened Abortion and Premature Labor," *Pacific Medicine and Surgery* 73 (1965): 382.

10. R. Squier and H. Dunbar, "Emotional Factors in the Course of Pregnancy," *Psychosomatic Medicine* 8 (1946): 161–175; E. Mann "Psychiatric Investigation of Habitual Abortion," *Obstetrics and Gynecology* 5 (1956): 589–601.

11. G. Peterson, "Prenatal Bonding, Prenatal Communication, and the Prevention of Prematurity," *Pre- and Perinatal Psychology Journal* 2:2 (1987): 89.

12. Ibid., pp. 89–90.

13. Ibid., pp. 88–89.

CHAPTER 9: THE METAMORPHOSIS OF CHILDBIRTH

1. E. Davis, *Women's Intuition* (Berkeley: Celestial Arts, 1989), p. 28.

2. N. Newton, "Interrelationships Between Sexual Responsiveness, Birth, and Breastfeeding," *Pre- and Perinatal Psychology Journal* 6:4 (1992): 317–36.

3. A. B. Kinsey, et al., *Sexual Behavior in the Human Female* (Philadelphia: Saunders, 1953), p. 86.

4. N. Newton, "Interrelationships Between Sexual Responsiveness, Birth, and Breastfeeding," *Pre- and Perinatal Psychology Journal* 6:4 (1992): 325.

5. E. Davis, *Women's Intuition* (Berkeley: Celestial Arts, 1989), p. 28.

6. C. Jones, *Mind Over Labor* (New York: Penguin, 1987), p. 13.

7. Adapted from the book *Mind Over Labor* by Carl Jones, (New York: Penguin, 1987), pp. 39–40.

8. M. Odent, *Birth Reborn*, (New York: Pantheon, 1984), pp. 45–47.

9. J. Kennell, M. Klaus, et al., "Continuous emotional support during labor in a U.S. hospital," *Journal of the American Medical Association* 265:17 (May 1991): 2197–2201.

10. R. Sosa, et al., "The Effectiveness of a Supportive Companion on Perinatal Problems, Length of Labor, and Mother-Infant Interaction," *New England Journal of Medicine* 303 (1980): 597–600.

11. Deborah A. Sullivan and Rose Weitz, *Labor Pains: Modern Midwives and Home Birth* (New Haven: Yale University Press, 1988), 112–32.

12. [R] D. Stewart, *The Five Standards for Safe Childbearing*, p.112, (Marble Hill, Mo.: NAPSAC reproductions 1981), pp. 122–23.

13. T. Montgomery, "A Case for Nurse-Midwives," *American Journal of Obstetrics and Gynecology* 1989): 50–58.

14. Bianca Gordon in Sheila Kitzinger and John A. David, *The Place of Birth* (New York: Oxford University Press, 1978), p. 201.

15. David Chamberlain, "Prenatal Intelligence," personal communication, 1993.

16. D. B. Chamberlain, "The Significance of Birth Memories," *Pre- and Perinatal Psychology*, 2:4 (1988): 221.

17. Ibid., pp. 214–15.

18. Ibid., p. 215.

19. S. McKay, "Shared Power: The Essence of Humanized Childbirth," *Pre- and Perinatal Psychology Journal* 5:4 (1991): 284.

20. Thomas Verny, *The Secret Life of the Unborn Child* (N.Y.: Delta, 1981), pp. 88–89.

21. M. H. Klaus and J. H. Kennel, *Maternal-Infant Bonding: The Impact of Early Separation or Loss on Family Development* (St. Louis: Mosby, 1976), pp. 33–34.

22. W. S. Condon and L. W. Sander, "Neonate Movement Is Synchronized with Adult Speech: Interactional Participation and Language Acquisition," *Science* 183 (1974): 99–101.

23. Ibid., pp. 99–101.

24. T. Kato, et al., "A Computer Analysis of Infant Movements Synchronized with Adult Speech," *Pediatric Research* 17 (1983): 625–28.

25. Barry M. Lester and C. F. Z. Boukydis, eds., *Infant Crying* (New York: Plenum, 1985), p. 53.

CHAPTER 10: DEVELOPING YOUR INTUITION

1. G. R. Schmeidler and R. A. McConnell, *ESP and Personality Patterns*, (New Haven, CT: Yale University Press, 1958), p. 16.

2. Weston Agor, "The Logic of Intuition: How Top Executives Make Important Decisions," *Organizational Dynamics* (1986): 12.

3. Ibid., p. 15.

4. E. Davis, *Women's Intuition* (Berkeley: Celestial Arts, 1989), pp. 37–38. The exercise "Running Energy" was adapted from her book.

5. E. Davis, *Women's Intuition* (Berkeley: Celestial Arts, 1989), pp. 49–51.

CHAPTER 11: INTUITION THAT OPENS DOORS

1. B. E. Schwarz, "Possible Telesomatic Reaction," *Journal of the Medical Society of New Jersey* 65:111 (November 1967): 600–03.

2. I. Stevenson, *Telepathic Impressions: A Review and Report of Thirty-Five New Cases* (Charlottesville: University Press of Virginia, 1970), p. 126.

3. Ibid., p. 128.

4. Ibid., pp. 27–28.

5. B. A. Ruggieri, "Pediatric Telepathy," *Corrective Psychiatry and Journal of Social Therapy*, 13:4 (1967): 187–95.

6. W. H. Trethowan and M. F. Conlon, "The Couvade Syndrome," *British Journal of Psychiatry* 111 (1965): 58–59.

7. E. Davis, *Women's Intuition* (Berkeley: Celestial Arts, 1989), p. 55.

8. C. M. Riley, "Teaching Mother/Fetus Communication: A Workshop on How To Teach Pregnant Mothers to Communicate with Their Unborn Children," *Pre- and Perinatal Psychology Journal* 3:2 (1988): 77–86.

9. C. M. Riley, "Transuterine Communication in Problem Pregnancies," *Pre- and Perinatal Psychology Journal* 1:3 (1987): 183.

10. H. H. Watkins, "Treating the Trauma of Abortion," *Pre- and Perinatal Psychology Journal* 1:2 (1986): 135–42.

11. Ibid., p. 137.

12. C. M. Riley, "Transuterine Communication in Problem Pregnancies," *Pre- and Perinatal Psychology Journal* 1:3 (1987): 183.

13. B. Grad, R. J. Cadoret, and G. I. Paul, "An Unorthodox Method of Treatment of Wound Healing in Mice," *International Journal of Parapsychology* 3:2 (1961): 5–24.

14. B. Grad, "A Telekinetic Effect on Plant Growth, II, Experiments Involving Treatment of Saline in Stoppered Bottles," *International Journal of Parapsychology* 6:4 (1964): 473–98.

15. *Parapsychology Review* 2:4 (1971): 12, cited in D. Scott Rogo, *Parapsychology: A Century of Inquiry*, (Taplinger Publishing, 1975), pp. 224–25.

CHAPTER 12: LOOKING AHEAD

1. Weston Agor, "The Logic of Intuition: How Top Executives Make Important Decisions," *Organizational Dynamics* (1986): 15.

2. Ibid.

3. Ibid.

4. H. Mintzberg, "Planning on the Left Side and Managing on the Right," *Harvard Business Review* (1976): pp. 49–58.

5. L. Harrison, *Anatomy of Reality: Merging of Intuition and Reason* (New York: Columbia University Press, 1983), p. 91.

6. L. Leshan, *The Medium, The Mystic, and the Physicist* (New York: Viking, 1974), p. 100.

7. Sir James Frazer, *The Golden Bough* (New York: New American Library.)

8. Ibid., p. 231.

9. Ibid., p. 232.

10. T. R. Verny, "Obstetrical Procedures: A Critical Examination of Their Effect on Pregnant Women and Their Unborn Children," *Pre- and Perinatal Psychology*, 7:2 (1992): 101.

11. Marsden G. Wagner "Infant Mortality in Europe: Implications for the United States," *Health Policy* (Winter, 1988): 473–84.

12. R. E. Davis-Floyd, "Obstetrical Rituals and Cultural Anomaly: Part II," *Pre- and Perinatal Psychology Journal* Vol 5:1 (1990): 35 [R].

13. R. Davis-Floyd, "Hospital Birth Routines as Rituals: Society's Messages to American Women," *Pre- and Perinatal Psychology Journal* 1:4 (1987): 278.

14. R. E. Davis-Floyd, "Obstetrical Rituals and Cultural Anomaly: Part I," *Pre- and Perinatal Psychology Journal* 4:3 (1990): 195.

15. R. Davis-Floyd, "Hospital Birth Routines as Rituals: Society's Messages to American Women," *Pre- and Perinatal Psychology Journal* 1:4 (1987): 293.

16. R. Davis-Floyd, "Obstetrical Rituals and Cultural Anomaly: Part II," *Pre- and Perinatal Psychology Journal* 5:1 (1990): 24.

17. David Banta and Stephen Thacker, "The Risks and Benefits of Episiotomies: A Review," *Birth* 9 (1982): 25–30.

18. H. Kantor, et al., "Value of Shaving the Pudendal-Perineal Area in Delivery Preparation," *Obstetrics and Gynecology* 25 (1965): 509–12.

19. Y. Liu, "Position During Labor and Delivery: History and Perspective," *Journal of Nurse-Midwifery* 24:3 (1979): 22.

20. Helen Varney, *Nurse-Midwifery* (Boston: Blackwell Scientific Publications, 1980), p. 353.

21. A. McBride, "Compulsory Rooming-in in the Ward and Private Newborn Service at Duke Hospital," *Journal of the American Medical Association* 145 (1983): 625.

22. M. Klaus and J. Kennell, "Mothers Separated From Their Newborn Infants," *Pediatric Clinics of North America* 17 (1970): 1015–1037.

23. D. B. Chamberlain, "The Significance of Birth Memories," *Pre- and Perinatal Psychology Journal* 2:4 (1988): 219.

24. Ibid., p. 217.

INDEX